THE

GOD

CHASERS

"My Soul Follows Hard After Thee"

THE
GOD
CHASERS

"My Soul Follows Hard After Thee"

TOMMY TENNEY

Dedication

This book is dedicated to my loving family: Jeannie, my wife of over 20 years, and my three daughters, Tiffany, Natasha, and Andrea, the earthly lights of my life and inspiration of much I hear from above. Thanks for "loaning out" Dad.

This book is also dedicated to God chasers everywhere— to pursuers of His presence. It is for them, the hungry, that this book was written. It could have been footnoted, annotated, and written for the analytical scholar. However, I purposely chose to write in a more conversational tone, style, and structure so that it might more easily whet the appetite, that some would "taste and see that the Lord is good."

Endorsements

"This book will light a living flame in your heart for the presence of God. Tommy Tenney opens his heart in a transparent cry for the Body of Christ to come into fresh relationship with their Savior. I must warn you, this is a dangerous book. If you are comfortable and complacent and want to stay that way, don't even open its pages!"

—Cindy Jacobs, Co-founder
Generals of Intercession

"God chasing is not a series of sprints. It goes the distance. Tommy Tenney shares his single-minded pursuit with the honesty of a disciple who is caught at last by His holy presence. Tommy will never be the same, nor will we who read and heed *The God Chasers*."

—Jane Hansen, President
Aglow International, Edmonds, Washington

"Every now and again a book appears on the shelves of Christian bookstores that has the potential to kill everyone who reads it. The God Chasers is not for the fainthearted but for those who, in the pursuit of God, are willing to die in the process. Tommy Tenney is such a man, continually dying in pursuit of God's presence. A life-changing read!"

—Ken Gott
Revival Now!, Sunderland, United Kingdom

"This book by Pastor Tommy Tenney will impact your life. I can completely identify with his message. It is a call to leave behind the average and the religiosity that walks without enthusiasm behind the Lord, to be a true pursuer of God—one who fights and is strengthened by reaching God and grasping His presence in a daily and constant way. The men and women whom God has used throughout history had different backgrounds and cultures, but He gave them all the same passion to know God and to walk with Him. Many years ago, my Christian life and my ministry were absolutely transformed by understanding this truth. If you long to live in a new spiritual stage of your life, if you want to raise yourself out of the shallow Christian routine to reach God in His present power and glory, without a doubt, this book is for you."

—Claudio Freidzon, Pastor
King of Kings Church, Buenos Aires, Argentina

"Are you a God chaser? Or is He chasing you? In Tommy Tenney's book *The God Chasers*, he provides immense help and insight for those dissatisfied with their level of devotion to Christ and their usefulness to others. Using biblical and contemporary heroes and heroines, this book will help sharpen the focus of every reader to embrace his or her destiny. We are living in momentous times; opportunities for the gospel abound. Only those chasing after God, His Word, and His Spirit will embrace that destiny. We either watch history or make it. Tommy Tenney's book will help us make some history at home, in the workplace, in society at large, and, for a few, in a national or international ministry."

—Gerald Coates, Speaker, Author, Broadcaster
Esher, Surrey, England

" 'But an hour is coming, and now is, when the true worshipers shall worship the Father in spirit and truth; for such people the Father seeks...' (Jn. 4:23 NAS). Tommy Tenney is a minister of the Holy Spirit and a demonstrator of God's power. Your eyes will tear and your heart beat with hunger as you join him in hot pursuit of the manifest presence of God."

—Bob Weiner, Founder
Weiner Ministries International and Maranatha Publications

"If you are looking for a 'Charismatic thrill' or instant 'fix,' you will not find them in this book. But if you will absorb this material, catch Tommy's spirit, and 'seek God's face,' you will be thrilled with the ultimate results. You will see the real Tommy Tenney emerge in *The God Chasers*. He defines much of the present 'Church system' as 'religious...but empty.' He says, 'You can be God's child and not have His favor,' and you instantly cry out in repentance, determined to have the favor of God on your life. The greatest thing I can tell you about this book is this: If you read it and give your attention to it, you will develop a hunger for God, and this hunger will start you on the road to glorious fulfillment. Why? Because if we hunger and thirst, we will be filled...with righteousness, with God! Read these pages and become a God chaser!"

—Charles Green, Pastor
Faith Church, New Orleans, Louisiana

"This book must be read by every Christian leader or anyone who wants to be a leader. It is a revelation of where God is taking the Church in the twenty-first century. Changes must begin *immediately*. Priorities *must* be in proper spiritual order...new paradigms for the new millennium. God must be *enthroned*, the *center*, the *absolute object* of our whole life.

"Tommy Tenney has captured the heartbeat of God concerning His plans and purposes and His desire for *intimacy* so He can empower those who enthrone Him. If this book is put into practice, it will result in both personal revival and corporate revival in all the churches of the world, and millions will be saved."

—Dr. Emanuele Cannistraci, Senior Pastor/Apostle
Evangel Christian Fellowship, San Jose, California

"It has been said that desperate days demand desperate measures. These times are not for those who seek a casual saunter toward God. *The God Chasers* are the order of the day. Jacob did not have time to build a bridge. Instead he availed himself of a midnight crossing, feeling his way along in pursuit of God. His wrestling match there at Jabbok changed his name, and changed him forever. We are living in a day that may culturally enjoy church as usual, but is screaming for a life-changing encounter with God. The journey and the apprehending must be personal. This book points you in the right direction. I commend my son, Tommy, and this book that matches the times."

—T.F. Tenney

"What Tommy writes in these pages, he lives every day. Not only is the heart of a man expressed in the pages of *The God Chasers*, but the heart of God is also expressed through the man. Tommy, in real life, every day, is a bona fide God chaser. May hearts be stirred to hunger and may they be overwhelmed with His love like never before as they read this much-needed book."

—Rev. Bart Pierce, Senior Pastor
Rock Church, Baltimore, Maryland

"There is a dimension beyond the anointing. When Aaron was anointed to be priest, he immediately turned and went into the presence of God and did not return for seven days. The anointing had prepared him to enter the glory realm.

"This is where I sense God is leading His people today. The focus of much recent teaching in the Church has been on the anointing. Now it is shifting to the glory of His presence.

"*The God Chasers* touches something deep within you as you read it. You find yourself being drawn to that dimension where Christ is calling us to enter—beyond the veil into His manifest presence."

—Richard Heard, Senior Pastor
Christian Tabernacle, Houston, Texas

"If someone was going to tell me how to find God...apprehend God...please God...enjoy God...and be changed by Him, I'd want it to be someone for whom it was a passionate and fruitful life quest. I have found that in Tommy Tenney, the man, and am grateful that he has given us a true blueprint for it in *The God Chasers*."

—Dr. Ché Ahn, Senior Pastor
Harvest Rock Church, Pasadena, California

"Tommy Tenney's testimony and writing can inspire your prayer life instantly—it did mine! There are some Christians who live their lives in cycles, experiencing both tremendous anointing and tremendous hunger for God. *The God Chasers* will challenge you to be one of them. If you dare to read it with an open heart, it will change your life."

—Rev. Sergio Scataglini, Senior Pastor
Puerta del Cielo (Door of Heaven Church)
La Plata, Argentina

"I have known Tommy Tenney all of my life, but when God tagged him, Tommy's ministry, life, and personality changed. If you do not want this Millennium change, then put this book down. I promise that you have never read anything like it. If you don't put this book down, you will become a chaser after God's real presence."

—Stephan K. Munsey, Pastor
Family Christian Center, Griffith, Indiana

"I first met Tommy Tenney almost four years ago at a pastor's conference in Beaumont, Texas. He was hungry for God—I recognized the look. It was the same one I had before going to Toronto a few months earlier. We prayed together, and didn't see each other for about two years. When I saw him again, he had found God in a very profound way—so much so that just listening to him appealed to something so deeply imbedded in our spirits that we were almost instantly in the presence of the One whom this man had been 'chasing.' This book will stir you to your deepest depths, and remind you of the original reason you first loved Him so much."

—Joseph L. Garlington, Pastor
Covenant Church, Pittsburgh, Pennsylvania

"I have been reading Tommy's book. I am alone in this room, but I am visibly shaken! I am caught up in the desire to know *Him*. I have been with Tommy and have witnessed his hunger for the Lord. I am challenged by his passion for His presence. Tommy's life has been life-changing to me. I will yet see God's glory. He is moving in our midst today. Read this book! Read it slowly! Become a God chaser!"

—Don Finto, Pastor
Belmont Church, Nashville, Tennessee

"This is a marvelous book on the wonderful danger of knowing God. *The God Chasers* is exciting, intense, unsettling, and challenging. Tommy holds no punches as he pleads with us to become desperate and determined in our pursuit of God."

—Ted Haggard, Senior Pastor
New Life Church, Colorado Springs, Colorado

"Through biblical examples and personal testimonies, Tommy Tenney exposes the deep ache that all true worshipers have—a longing for the very presence of God Himself. An 'average' or mediocre relationship with the Lord will not do; we must have more of the Spirit of God!"

—Larry Stockstill, Pastor
Bethany World Prayer Center

"I challenge every minister of the gospel to take two days alone with God and this book. Allow it to birth a 'cry' within you—not for the latest spiritual 'fad,' but for God Himself. Tommy Tenney deals with the Church's most crucial need: a fresh visitation of God's presence. Read it and pass it on."

—David Ravenhill
Author of *For God's Sake Grow Up!*

"This book by Tommy Tenney is truly a passionate and motivating message for the Church. Its theme is simple: that we might seek the face of God and His glory. In a variety of ways, using Scripture and illustrations, Rev. Tenney seeks to open our eyes to what he sees: a life lived in the presence of the Spirit; a life of transforming power;

a life of delighting in Him, Jesus the Messiah! Why would we be denied or accept anything less than the promise so well reflected in this book?"

—Daniel Juster, Th.D.
Director, Tikkun Ministries

"Indeed, this book feels like a 'fireside chat' that comes from the heart of the author, it is so personal, real, and warm. It really touches the hearts of all who desire to have an intimate relationship with Jesus. And it is extremely readable, just like listening to Tommy in person. I would recommend this book without reservation not only to all who long to experience more of Jesus than mere 'Christianity,' but also to my fellow ministers who seek after God rather than the ministry."

—Ernest Chan, President
Agape Renewal Center

"All of us desire revival, but only God can bring it. Even though we cannot schedule or program a revival, we can follow the biblical way of repentance, holy living, and constancy in expecting revival. Tommy Tenney's book, *The God Chasers*, is more than a primer for revival; it will compel us to pursue God with the goal of revival. It is a must-read for all who eagerly await to see revival in our time."

—Rev. Felix Liu, Senior Pastor
Evangelical Formosan Church of Los Angeles

"Generation after generation, people serve God either by tradition or duty; yet, in every generation comes those who go beyond just "needing" God. They develop a want and a hunger for God, throwing their lives into seeking Him. They are "rare seekers" who are in search of a place to worship and minister to the Lord in spirit and truth. Tommy Tenney is an example of one who has gone beyond needing God to one who wants Him with all his

14

being. This shows in his life. I highly endorse Tommy's book, *The God Chasers*. I believe it is one of the most powerful books of the century and will separate followers and admirers from true disciples."

—Kingsley A. Fletcher, Senior Pastor
Life Community Church
Research Triangle Park, North Carolina

No one can write a book this dynamic and life-changing unless he or she has had a life-changing encounter with God. Tommy Tenney puts into words what I have felt for so long—that the insatiable hunger for more of God is not only normal, it's the way God wants us to feel. He wants us to pursue Him until He catches us. Once we've had that extraordinary glimpse of Him, we will stop at nothing to be able to behold Him in all His fullness.

—Sturmie Omartian
Best-selling author

Contents

Introduction

There Have Always Been God Chasers

As long as there has been God, there have been God chasers. History is filled with their stories. Mine is just another. Stories of this type can be read as road maps to the Holy of Holies, or to places of access to the heavenlies.

God chasers transcend time and culture. They come from every background imaginable. They come from every era of time that has existed...from Abraham the wandering herdsman, to Moses the adopted stutterer, to David the shepherd boy. As the parade of time continues, the names keep popping up: Madame Jeanne Guyon, Evan Roberts, William Seymour of Azusa Street fame—until we reach today. Really, only history can tell us the names of God chasers, but they're there. Are you one? God is just waiting to be caught by someone whose hunger exceeds his grasp.

God chasers have a lot in common. Primarily, they are not interested in camping out on some dusty truth

19

known to everyone. They are after the fresh presence of the Almighty. Sometimes their pursuit raises the eyebrows of the existing church, but usually they lead the church from a place of dryness back into the place of His presence. If you're a God chaser, you won't be happy to simply follow God's tracks. You will follow them *until you apprehend His presence.*

The difference between the truth of God and revelation is very simple. Truth is where God's *been.* Revelation is where God is. Truth is God's tracks. It's His trail, His path, but it leads to what? It leads to Him. Perhaps the masses of people are happy to know where God's been, but true God chasers are not content just to study God's trail, His truths; they want to *know* Him. They want to know where He is and what He's doing right now.

Sadly, today the bulk of the Church is like some proverbial detective holding a magnifying glass in his hand and studying where God has been. Of course, a hunter can determine a lot by studying the tracks of an animal. He can determine which direction it's going, how long it has been since it passed there, how much it weighs, whether it is male or female, and so on. Unfortunately, the Church today spends countless hours and much energy debating where God has been, how heavy He was when He was there, and even His gender. To true God chasers, all these things are immaterial. They want to run hard and hot on this trail of truth until they arrive at the point of revelation, where He presently exists.

A God chaser may be excited about some dusty truth, and may even be thrilled somewhat over determining the weight of the *kabod,* or glory, that passed in the path, and how long ago it was. But that's just the problem. How long ago was it? A true God chaser is not happy with just past truth; he must have *present* truth. God chasers don't want to just study from the moldy pages of what God has done; they're anxious to see what God is doing.

There is a vast difference between present truth and past truth.[1] I'm afraid that most of what the Church has studied is past truth, and very little of what we know is present truth.

If you want to recognize a real God chaser, think of a whooping, barking, tail-pounding dog trembling with excitement. Just give God chasers the scent that God is nearby and see what happens. As the Bible says, the scent of water causes many things to happen.[2] Like bloodhounds on a trail, they'll get most excited when they reach their prey. In this instance, their prey is His presence.

All I can say is, I'm a God chaser. And so are a lot of those who have had God encounters. Why don't you come join the company of God chasers?

We just want to be with Him.

Introduction to "notes from those on the chase"

*I*n November of 1998, the first *The God Chasers* book came off the press. Even though we knew that this was a great book and we were certain it would deeply impact the Body of Christ, we have been overwhelmed at the influence it has had around the world.

The God Chaser phrase has been integrated into the structure of Christian communication and fittingly describes those individuals whose hearts long for encounters with the living God.

Since that first printing over 1.5 million copies of *The God Chasers* has come off the press and it has been translated in 20 languages including Spanish, French, German, Arabic, and Hebrew.

The God Chasers first entered the **Top 20 Bestseller's List** in August 1999 and remains there till present.

Thousands of letters have been written from people around the world whose hearts have been touched by the passionate words of Tommy Tenney. Because our hearts have been moved by these letters we thought that you would also enjoy reading some of those letters. So we have including a sampling of those letters for your enjoyment and inspiration.

Because so many people are using *The God Chasers* in Bible studies we have also including a study guide at the end of each chapter.

We are happy to present to you this beautifully designed casebound *Collector's Edition* and trust that you will cherish it as you did you very first *God Chasers* book.

—Don Nori
Publisher

Endnotes

1. See 2 Pet. 1:12.
2. See Job 14:9.

Chapter 1

THE DAY I
ALMOST CAUGHT HIM

Running hard after God—Ps. 63:8

We think we know where God lives.

We think we know what He likes, and we are *sure* we know what He dislikes.

We have studied God's Word and His old love letters to the churches so much that some of us claim to know *all* about God. But now people like you and me around the world are beginning to hear a voice speak to them with persistent but piercing repetition in the stillness of the night:

"I'm not asking you how much you know *about* Me; I want to ask you, 'Do you really *know* Me? Do you really *want* Me?' "

I thought I did. At one time I thought I had achieved a good measure of success in the ministry. After all, I had preached in some of the largest churches in America. I was involved in international outreach efforts with great men of God. I went to Russia numerous times and helped start many churches there. I've done a lot of things *for* God... because I thought that was what I was supposed to do.

But on one autumn Sunday morning, something happened to change all that. It put all my ministerial accomplishments, credentials, and achievements in jeopardy. A long-time friend of mine who pastored a church in Houston, Texas, had asked me to speak at his church. I somehow sensed that destiny was waiting. Prior to his call, a hunger had been birthed in my heart that just wouldn't go away. The gnawing vacuum of emptiness in the midst of my accomplishments just got worse. I was in a frustrating funk, a divine depression of destiny. When he called I just sensed that something awaited us from God. Little did we know that we were approaching a divine appointment.

I am a fourth generation Spirit-filled Christian, three generations deep into ministry, but I must be honest with you: I was sick of church. I was just like most of the people we try to lure into our services every week. They won't come because they are sick of church too. But on the other hand, though most of the people who drive by our churches, live within sight of our steeples, and inhabit our meeting halls may be sick of church as well, they're also *hungry for God*.

"Somewhat Less Than Advertised"

*Y*ou can't tell me they're not hungry for God when they wear crystals around their necks, lay down hundreds of dollars a day to listen to gurus, and call psychics to the tune of billions of dollars per year. They're hungry to hear from something that's beyond themselves, something they are not hearing in the Church of today. The bottom line is that people are sick of church because the Church has been somewhat less than what the Book advertised! *People want to connect with a higher power!* Their hunger drives them to everywhere but the Church. They search in pursuits of the flesh to try to feed the hunger that gnaws at their souls.

Ironically, as a minister I was suffering from the same hunger pangs as the people who had never met Jesus before! I just wasn't content to know *about* Jesus anymore. You can know all about presidents, royalties, and celebrities; you can know their eating habits, address, and marital status. But knowing about them doesn't imply intimacy. That doesn't mean you *know* them. In this information age, with tidbits of gossip passed from mouth to mouth, from paper to paper, and from person to person, it's possible to traffic in facts about someone without knowing him personally. Were you to overhear two people conversing about the latest calamity befalling some celebrity, or the latest victory he experienced, you might be led to think that they know that individual, when really all they know is facts about him! For too long the Church has been only conversant in the *things* of God. We talk techniques, but we don't talk with Him. That's the difference between knowing someone and knowing about him. Presidents, royalties, and celebrities—I may know many facts about them, but I don't really *know* them. If I ever met them in person, they would have to be introduced to me because mere knowledge about a person is not the same as an intimate friendship.

It's simply not enough to know about God. We have churches filled with people who can win Bible trivia contests but who don't *know* Him. I am afraid that some of us have been sidetracked or entangled by everything from prosperity to poverty, and we've become such an ingrown society of the self-righteous that *our* desires and *our* wants and those of the *Holy Spirit* are two different matters.

If we're not careful, we can become so interested in developing the "cult of the comfortable" with our comfortable pastor, our comfortable church building, and our comfortable circle of friends, that we forget about the thousands of discontented, wounded, and dying people who pass by our comfortable church every day! I can't help but think that if we fail to even try to reach them with the gospel of Jesus Christ, then *He sure wasted a lot of blood on Calvary.* Now *that* makes *me* uncomfortable.

There had to be more. I was desperate for a God encounter (of the closest kind).

I returned home after speaking at my friend's church in Texas. The following Wednesday, as I was standing in the kitchen, the pastor called again. He said, "Tommy, we've been friends for years now. And I don't know that I've ever asked anybody to come back for a second Sunday in a row...but would you come back here next Sunday too?" I agreed. We could tell that *God was up to something.* Was the pursuer now being pursued? Were we about to be apprehended by that which we ourselves were chasing?[1]

This second Sunday was even more intense. No one wanted to leave the building after the Sunday night service.

"What should we do?" my pastor friend asked.

"We should have a prayer meeting on Monday night," I said, "with no other agenda. Let's gauge the hunger of the people and see what's happening." Four hundred people showed up that Monday for the prayer meeting, and all we did was seek the face of God. Something was definitely going on. A minuscule crack was appearing in the brass heavens over the city of Houston. Collective hunger was crying for a corporate visitation.

I went back home and by Wednesday the pastor was on the phone again, saying, "Tommy, can you come back again for Sunday?" I heard past his words and listened to his heart. He really was not interested in "me" coming back. What he and I both wanted was God. He is a fellow God chaser and we were in hot pursuit. His church had fueled a flaming hunger in me. They too had been preparing for pursuit. There was a sense that we were close to "catching" Him.

That's an interesting phrase, isn't it? *Catching Him.* Really, it's an impossible phrase. We can no more catch Him than the east can catch the west; they're too far removed from each other. It's like playing chase with my daughter. Often as she arrives home from a day of school, we play this little game that countless fathers and children play around the world. When she comes and tries to catch me, even with my hulking frame, I really don't have to run. I just artfully dodge this way and then that, and she can't even touch me, because a six-year-old can't catch an adult. But that's not really the purpose of the game, because a few minutes into it, she laughingly says, "Oh daddy," and it's at that moment that she captures my heart, if not my presence or body. And then I turn and she's no longer chasing me, but I'm chasing her, and I catch her and we tumble in the grass with hugs and kisses. The pursuer becomes the pursued. So can we catch Him? Not really, but we can catch His heart. David did. And if we catch His heart, then He turns and chases us. That's the beauty of being a God chaser. You're chasing the impossible, knowing it's possible.

This body of believers in Houston had two scheduled services on Sundays. The first morning service started at 8:30, and the second one followed and began at 11.

When I returned for the third weekend, while in the hotel, I sensed a heavy anointing of some kind, a brooding of the Spirit, and I literally wept and trembled.

You Could Barely Breathe

The following morning, we walked into the building for the 8:30 Sunday service expecting to see the usual early morning first service "sleepy" crowd with their low-key worship. As I walked in to sit down in the front row that morning, the presence of God was already in that place so heavily that the air was "thick." You could barely breathe.

The musicians were clearly struggling to continue their ministry; their tears got in the way. Music became more difficult to play. Finally, the presence of God hovered so strongly that they couldn't sing or play any longer. The worship leader crumpled in sobs behind the keyboard.

If there was one good decision I made in life, it was made that day. I had never been this close to "catching" God, and I was not going to stop. So I spoke to my wife, Jeannie. "You should go continue to lead us to Him." Jeannie has an anointing to lead people into the presence of God as a worshiper and intercessor. She quietly moved to the front and continued to facilitate the worship and ministry to the Lord. It wasn't anything fancy; it was just simple. That was the only appropriate response in that moment.

The atmosphere reminded me of the passage in Isaiah 6, something I'd read about, and even dared dream I might experience myself. In this passage the glory of the Lord filled the temple. I'd never understood what it meant for the glory of the Lord to fill a place. I had sensed God come in places, I had sensed Him come by, but this time in Houston, even after there was all of God that I thought was available in the building, more of His presence literally packed itself into the room. It's like the bridal train of a bride that, after she has personally entered the building, her bridal train continues to enter the building after her. God was there; of that there was no doubt. But more of Him kept coming in the place until, as in Isaiah, it literally filled the building. At times the air was so rarefied that it became almost unbreathable. Oxygen came in short gasps, seemingly. Muffled sobs broke through the room. In the midst of this, the pastor turned to me and asked me a question.

"Tommy, are you ready to take the service?"

"Pastor, I'm just about half-afraid to step up there, because *I sense that God is about to do something.*"

Tears were streaming down my face when I said that. I wasn't afraid that God was going to strike me down, or that something bad was going to happen. I just didn't want to interfere and grieve the precious presence that was filling up that room! For too long we humans have only allowed the Holy Spirit to take control *up to a certain point.* Basically, whenever it gets outside of our comfort zone or just a little beyond our control, we pull in the reins (the Bible calls it "quenching the Spirit" in First Thessalonians 5:19). We stop at the tabernacle veil too many times.

"I feel like I should read Second Chronicles 7:14, and I have a word from the Lord," my pastor friend said.

With profuse tears I nodded assent and said, "Go, go."

My friend is not a man given to any kind of outward demonstration; he is essentially a man of "even" emotions.

But when he got up to walk to the platform, he appeared visibly shaky. At this point I so sensed something was about to happen, that I walked all the way from the front row to the back of the room to stand by the sound booth. I knew God was going to do something; I just didn't know where. I was on the front row, and it could happen behind me or to the side of me. I was so desperate to catch Him that I got up and publicly walked back to the sound booth as the pastor walked up to the pulpit to speak, so I could see whatever happened. I wasn't even sure that it was going to happen on the platform, but I knew something was going to happen. "God, I want to be able to see whatever it is You are about to do."

My pastor friend stepped up to the clear[2] pulpit in the center of the platform, opened the Bible, and quietly read the gripping passage from Second Chronicles 7:14:

If My people, which are called by My name, shall humble themselves, and pray, and seek My face, and turn from their wicked ways; then will I hear from heaven, and will forgive their sin, and will heal their land.

Then he closed his Bible, gripped the edges of the pulpit with trembling hands, and said, "The word of the Lord to us is to stop seeking His benefits and seek Him. We are not to seek His hands any longer, but seek His face."

In that instant, I heard what sounded like a thunderclap echo through the building, and the pastor was literally picked up and thrown backward about ten feet, effectively separating him from the pulpit. When he went backward, the pulpit fell forward. The beautiful flower arrangement positioned in front of it fell to the ground, but *by the time the pulpit hit the ground*, it was already in two pieces. It had split into two pieces almost as if lightning had hit it! At that instant the tangible terror of the presence of God filled that room.

People Began to Weep and Wail

I quickly stepped to the microphone from the back of the room and said, "In case you aren't aware of it, God has just moved into this place. The pastor is fine. [It was two and a half hours before he could even get up, though—and even then the ushers had to carry him. Only his hand trembled slightly to give proof of life.] He's going to be fine."

While all of this happened, the ushers quickly ran to the front to check on the pastor and to pick up the two pieces of the split pulpit. No one really paid much attention to the split pulpit; we were too occupied with the torn heavenlies. The presence of God had hit that place like some kind of bomb. People began to weep and to wail. I said, "If you're not where you need to be, this is a good time to get right with God." I've never seen such an altar call. It was pure pandemonium. People shoved one another out of the way. They wouldn't wait for the aisles to clear; they climbed over pews, businessmen tore their ties off, and they were literally stacked on top of one another, in the most horribly harmonious sound of repentance you ever heard. Just the thought of it still sends chills down my back. When I gave the altar call then for the 8:30 a.m. service, I had no idea that it would be but the first of seven altar calls that day.

When it was time for the 11:00 service to begin, nobody had left the building. The people were still on their faces and, even though there was hardly any music being played at this point, worship was rampant and uninhibited. Grown men were ballet dancing; little children were weeping in repentance. People were on their faces, on their feet, on their knees, but mostly in His presence. There was so much of the presence and the power of God there that people began to feel an urgent need to be baptized. I watched people walk through the doors of repentance, and one after another experienced the glory and the presence of God as He came near. Then they wanted baptized, and I was in a quandary about what to do. The pastor was still unavailable on the floor. Prominent people walked up to me and stated, "I've got to be baptized. Somebody tell me what to do." They joined with the parade of the unsaved, who were now saved, provoked purely by encountering the presence of God. There was no sermon and no real song—just His Spirit that day.

Two and a half hours had passed, and since the pastor had only managed to wiggle one finger at that point to call the elders to him, the ushers had carried him to his office. Meanwhile, all these people were asking me (or anyone else they could find) if they could be baptized. As a visiting minister at the church, I didn't want to assume the authority to tell anyone to baptize these folks, so I sent people back to the pastor's office to see if he would authorize the water baptisms.

I gave one altar call after another, and hundreds of people were coming forward. As more and more people came to me asking about water baptism, I noticed that no one I had sent to the pastor's office had returned. Finally I sent a senior assistant pastor back there and told him, "Please find out what Pastor wants to do about the water baptisms—nobody has come back to tell me yet." The man stuck his head in the pastor's office, and to his shock he saw the pastor still lying before the Lord, and everyone I had sent there was sprawled on the floor too, just weeping and repenting before God. He hurried back to tell me what he had seen and added, "I'll go ask him, but if I go in that office I may not be back either."

We Baptized People for Hours

I shrugged my shoulders and agreed with the associate pastor, "I guess it's all right to baptize them." So we began to baptize people as a physical sign of their repentance before the Lord, and we ended up baptizing people for hours. More and more people kept pouring in, and since the people from the early service were still there, there were cars parked everywhere outside the church building. A big open-air ball field next to the building was filled with cars parked every which way.

As people drove onto the parking lot, they sensed the presence of God so strongly that some began to weep uncontrollably. They just found themselves driving up onto the parking lot or into the grass not knowing what was going on. Some started to get out of their cars and barely managed to stagger across the parking lot. Some came inside the building only to fall to the floor just inside the doors. The hard-pressed ushers had to literally pull the helpless people away from the doors and stack them up along the walls of the hallways to clear the entrance. Others managed to make it partway down the hallways, and some made it to the foyer before they fell on their faces in repentance.

Some actually made it inside the auditorium, but most of them didn't bother to find seats. They just made for the altar. No matter what they did or how far they made it, it wasn't long before they began to weep and repent. As I said, there wasn't any preaching. There wasn't even any music part of the time. Primarily one thing happened that day: The presence of God showed up. When that happens, the first thing you do is the same thing Isaiah did when he saw the Lord high and lifted up. He cried out from the depths of his soul:

Then said I, Woe is me! for I am undone; because I
am a man of unclean lips, and I dwell in the midst
of a people of unclean lips: for mine eyes have seen
the King, the Lord of hosts (Isaiah 6:5).

You see, the instant Isaiah the prophet, the chosen servant of God, saw the King of glory, what he used to think was clean and holy now looked like filthy rags. He was thinking, I thought I knew God, but I didn't know this much of God! That Sunday we seemed to come so close; we almost caught Him. Now I know it's possible.

They Came Right Back for More

People just kept filling the auditorium again and again, beginning with that strange service that started at 8:30 that morning. I finally went to eat at around 4:00 that afternoon, and then came right back to the church building. Many never left. The continuous "Sunday morning service" lasted until 1:00 Monday morning. We didn't have to announce our plans for Monday evening. Everybody already knew. Frankly, there would have been a meeting whether we announced it or not. The people simply went home to get some sleep or do the things they had to do, and they came right back for more—not for more of men and their programs, but for God and His presence.

Night after night, the pastor and I would come in and say, "What are we going to do?"

Most of the time our answer to one another was just as predictable: "What do you want to do?"

What we meant was, "I don't know what to do. What does He want to do?"

Sometimes we'd go in and start trying to "have church," but the crying hunger of the people would quickly draw in the presence of God and suddenly *God had us!*

Listen, my friend, God doesn't care about your music, your midget steeples, and your flesh-impressive buildings. Your church carpet doesn't impress Him—He carpets the fields. God doesn't really care about anything you can "do" for Him; He only cares about your answer to one question: "*Do you want Me?*"

Ruin Everything That Isn't of You, Lord!

We have programmed our church services so tightly that we really don't leave room for the Holy Spirit. Oh, we might let God speak prophetically to us a little, but we get nervous if He tries to break out of our schedules. We can't let God out of the box too much because He can ruin everything. (That has become my prayer: "Break out of our boxes, Lord, and ruin everything that isn't of You!")

Let me ask you a question: How long has it been since you came to church and said, "We are going to wait on the Lord"? I think we are afraid to wait on Him because we're afraid He won't show up. I have a promise for you: "They that wait upon the Lord shall renew their strength" (Is. 40:31a). Do you want to know why we've lived in weakness as Christians and have not had all that God wanted for us? Do you want to know why we have lived beneath our privilege and have not had the strength to overcome our own carnality? Maybe it's because we haven't waited on Him to show up to empower us, and we're trying to do too much in the power of our own soulish realm.

God Ruined Everything in Houston

I am not trying to make you feel bad. I know most Christians and most of our leaders genuinely mean well, but *there is so much more.* You can "catch" God—ask Jacob—and it might ruin the way you've

39

always walked! But you can catch Him. We've talked, preached, and taught about revival until the Church is sick of hearing about it. That's what I did for a living: I preached revivals—or so I thought. Then God broke out of His box and *ruined everything* when He showed up. Seven nights a week, for the next four or five weeks straight, hundreds of people a night would stand in line to repent and receive Christ, worship, wait, and pray. What had happened in history, past and present, was happening again. Then it dawned on me, "God, You're wanting to do this *everywhere.*" For months His manifest presence hovered.

God Is Coming Back to Repossess the Church

As far as I can tell, there is only one thing that stops Him. He is not going to pour out His Spirit where He doesn't find hunger. He looks for the hungry. Hunger means you're dissatisfied with *the way it has been* because it forced you to live without *Him* in His fullness. He only comes when you are ready to turn it all over to Him. God is coming back to repossess His Church, but you have to be hungry.

He wants to reveal Himself among us. He wants to come ever stronger, and stronger, and stronger, and stronger *until your flesh won't be able to stand it.* The beauty of it is this: *neither will the unsaved driving by* be able to resist. It's beginning to happen. I have seen the day when sinners veer off the highway when they drive by places of an open heaven. They pull into parking lots with puzzled looks, and they knock on the doors and say, "Please, there's something here...I've got to have it."

What Do We Do?

Aren't you tired of trying to pass out tracts, knock on doors, and make things happen?

We've been trying to make things happen for a long time. Now *He* wants to make it happen! Why don't you find out what He's doing and join in? That's what Jesus did. He said, "Father, what are You doing? That's what I'll do."[5]

God wants to move in with your church family. How long has it been since you've been so hungry for God that it consumed you to the point where you couldn't care less what people thought of you? I challenge you right now to forget about every distraction, every opinion, but one. What are you feeling right now as you read about how God Himself invaded these churches? Are you squelching it? What is gripping your heart? Don't you feel the awakening of what you thought was a long-dead hunger? How long has it been since you felt what you're feeling right now? Rise up and pursue His presence. Become a God chaser.

I'm not talking about the excitement of praise and worship, as we would call it. We know how to get the music "just right" so the singing is stunning, the accompaniment is awesome, and everything seems perfect. But that's not what I'm talking about, and that's not what is causing your hunger right now. I'm talking about a hunger for *God's presence.* I said "a hunger for *God's presence.*"

Let me be blunt for a moment. I know in my heart of hearts that the truth of the matter is this: The Church has lived in self-righteous smugness for so long that we stink in God's nostrils. He can't even look at us in our present state. In the same way that you or I might feel embarrassed in a restaurant or grocery store when we see someone's children acting up and getting away with it, God feels the same way about our self-righteousness. God is uncomfortable with our smug self-righteousness. We are not "as together" as we think we are.

"What causes this kind of thing to happen?"

"Repentance."

In those days came John the Baptist, preaching in the wilderness of Judaea,

*And saying, **Repent ye: for the kingdom of heaven is at hand.***

*For this is he that was spoken of by the prophet Esaias, saying, The voice of one crying in the wilderness, **Prepare ye the way of the Lord, make His paths straight*** (Matthew 3:1-3).

Repentance prepares the way and makes the road of our hearts straight. Repentance builds up every low place and takes down every high place in our lives and church families. *Repentance prepares us for His presence.* In fact, you cannot live in His presence without repentance. Repentance permits pursuit of His presence. It builds the road for you to get to God (or for God to get to you!). Just ask John the Baptist. When he built the road, Jesus "came walking."

This is the crux of what I have to say: How long has it been since you said, "I'm going for God"? How long has it been since you laid aside everything that ever occupied you and ran down the road of repentance to *pursue God?*

It's Not a Pride Thing; It's a Hunger Thing

I used to pursue preaching good sermons and great crowds, and attempt great accomplishments for Him. But I've been ruined. Now I'm a God chaser. Nothing else matters anymore. I tell you that as your brother in Christ, I love you. But I love Him more. I couldn't care less about what other people or ministers think about me. I'm going after God. That's not a pride thing; it's a *hunger* thing. When you pursue God with all your heart, soul, and body, He will turn to meet you and you will come out of it *ruined* for the world.

Good things have become the enemy of the best things. I challenge you and release you right now as you read these words to let your heart be broken by the Holy Ghost. It's time for you to make your life holy. Quit watching what you used to watch; quit reading what you used to read if you are reading it more than you read His Word. He must be your first and greatest hunger.

If you are contented and satisfied, then I'll leave you alone and you can safely put down this book at this point and I won't ever bother you again. But if you are hungry, I have a promise from the Lord for you. He said, "Blessed are they which do hunger and thirst after righteousness: for they shall be filled" (Mt. 5:6).

We Have Never Been Hungry

Our problem is that we have never really been hungry. We have allowed things of this realm to satisfy our lives and satiate our hunger. We have come to God week after week, year after year, just to have Him fill in the little empty spaces. I tell you that God is tired of being "second place" to everything else in our lives. He is even tired of being second to the local church program and church life!

Everything good, including the things your local church does—from feeding the poor, to rescuing babies at the pregnancy counseling center, to teaching kids in the Sunday school classes—should flow from the presence of God. Our primary motivating factor should be, "We do it because of Him and because it is His heart." But if we're not careful, we can get so caught up in doing things *for* Him that we forget about *Him*.

You can get so caught up in being "religious" that you never become spiritual. It doesn't matter how much you pray. (Pardon me for saying this, but you can be lost, not

43

even knowing God, and still have a prayer life.) I don't care how much you know about the Bible, or what you know *about* Him. I'm asking you, "Do you *know Him?*"

I'm afraid that we have satiated our hunger for Him by reading old love letters from Him to the churches in the Epistles of the New Testament. These are good, holy, and necessary, but we never have intimacy with Him. We have stifled our hunger for His presence by doing things for Him.

A husband and wife can do things *for* each other while never really loving each other. They can go through childbirth classes together, have kids, and share a mortgage, but never enjoy the *high level of intimacy* that God ordained and designed for a marriage (and I'm not just talking about sexual things). Too often we live on a lower plane than what God intended for us, so when He unexpectedly shows up in His power, we are shocked. Most of us are simply not prepared to see "His train fill the temple."

The Holy Spirit may already be speaking to you. If you are barely holding back the tears, then let them go. I ask the Lord, right now, to awaken an old, old hunger that you have almost forgotten. Perhaps you used to feel this way in days gone by, but you've allowed other things to fill you up and replace that desire for His presence.

In Jesus' name, I release you from dead religion into spiritual hunger, this very moment. I pray that you get so hungry for God that you don't care about anything else.

I think I see a flickering flame. *He* will "fan" that.

Lord, we just want Your presence. We are so hungry.

❧ Notes from those on the chase ❧

*My name is Richard H., and I am the pastor of a Baptist church in England. I have just finished reading **The God Chasers** and have started reading **The God Catchers**. Rarely has any book grabbed my attention so much so that I could hardly put it down until I had finished it! There is a queue [line] in my family to read it, but I want to read it again and again. I try to avoid overusing such phrases as "anointed," but **The God Catchers** is anointed! It delivered a number of spiritual thunderbolts into my own life. Ouch! I look forward to the fire spreading through the rest of our fellowship and across our city! It speaks powerfully to my heart and desire. I am still trying to work it out in my life, and it has gotten me excited again! It has gotten me to lift my head again. God bless you all, keep up the excellent work!*

—Richard H.

❧   ❧

I just finished your first book, (I saw you and your wife on Brother Hinn's TV crusade.) WOW. Tough book to read through, brother! I was so moved when I read about the Lord our God showing up at that church. I pray for that a lot and agree with you that all of us must humble ourselves and repent before a revival can happen in this country.

After I started to read your book about that very thing, I just started to pray for it on the way to work. (I leave early every morning to drive to work, and I spend that time in prayer and thanksgiving.) I just started to tell the Lord that I just wanted to love and seek Him more. I did that for about a week after I started reading your book and He visited me right there in my truck while I was driving. Well, it was pretty tough to keep driving and have the Lord there speaking to my heart (I was weeping, and it was hard to breathe, too). I should have stopped, but I didn't want the Lord to leave either. This went on for about 30 minutes until I got to work where I just sat in my truck, having been covered by the Lord. I have never, ever had that happen to me before. I have in the past repented and wept before the Lord in repentance, and I know that He was there to forgive me. But this was different...I just did not want Him to leave. I was still overcome by His presence. (I know what you mean, Brother Tenney; you are never the same.) I just want more of Him.

—Mike N.

Understanding the chase for the Lord

1. What is the difference between knowing *about* God and actually *knowing* God? What is the difference between serving God and having a relationship with Him?

2. How did you initially get to know the Lord? How did you get to your present place of knowing Him?

3. What does it mean to be hungry for God? What encourages people to be hungry for Him? What encourages you to be hungry for Him?

4. What does it mean to seek God's face and not His hand? Do you seek His face every day? Why or why not?

Endnotes

1. See Phil. 3:12.

2. The pulpit was made of a high-tech acrylic plastic, often mistakenly called plexiglas. This material was said by engineers to be able to withstand tens of thousands of pounds of pressure per square inch.

3. See Jn. 5:19-20.

Chapter 2

NO BREAD IN THE "HOUSE OF BREAD"

Crumbs in the carpet and empty shelves

The priority of God's presence has been lost in the modern Church. We're like bakeries that are open, but have no bread. And furthermore, we're not interested in selling bread. We just like the chit-chat that goes on around cold ovens and empty shelves. In fact, I wonder, do we even know whether He's here or not, and if He is here, what He's doing? Where He is going? Or are we just too preoccupied with sweeping out imaginary crumbs from bakeries with no bread?

Do We Even Know When He's in Town?

On the day Jesus made what we call His triumphant entry into Jerusalem on the back of a little donkey, His path through the city probably led Him right past the entrance to the temple of Herod. I believe the reason the Pharisees were upset at the parade in John

12 is because it disturbed their religious services inside the temple.

I can hear them complaining, "What is all this going on? You're disturbing the high priest! Don't you know what we are doing? We are having a very important prayer service inside. Do you know what we're praying for? *We're praying for the Messiah to come!* And you have the audacity to have this noisy parade and disturb us?! Who is in charge of this unruly mob anyway?"

Uh, do you see the guy on the little donkey?

They missed the hour of their visitation. He was in town and they didn't know it. The Messiah passed right by their door while they were inside praying for Him to come. The problem was that He didn't come in the manner in which they expected Him to come. They didn't recognize Him. Had Jesus come on the back of a prancing white stallion, or in a royal chariot of gold with a phalanx of soldiers ahead of Him, the Pharisees and priests would have said, "That might be Him." Unfortunately, they were more interested in seeing the Messiah throw off the yoke of Roman bondage than in throwing off the spiritual bondage that had become a blight on their land and people.

God is getting ready to break out in America, even if He has to bypass her stuffy churches to break out in the barrooms! We would be wise to remember that He has bypassed the religious elite before to dine with the poor, the profane, and the prostitutes. The Western Church, and the American Church in particular, has exported its programs about God all over the world, but it is time for us to learn that our *programs* are not progress. What we need is His *presence.* We need to decide that whatever it takes and wherever it comes from, we must have Him. And He wants to come—on His terms, not ours. Until then, the absence of "awesomeness" will haunt the Church.

We can be *inside* praying for Him to come while He passes by *outside*. Worse than that, the "insiders" miss Him while the "outsiders" march with Him!

Bread Is Scarce During Times of Famine

N *ow it came to pass in the days when the judges ruled, that **there was a famine in the land**. And a certain man of **Bethlehemjudah**[1] went to sojourn in the country of Moab, he, and his wife, and his two sons.*

And the name of the man was Elimelech, and the name of his wife Naomi, and the name of his two sons Mahlon and Chilion, Ephrathites of Bethlehemjudah. And they came into the country of Moab, and continued there.

And Elimelech Naomi's husband died; and she was left, and her two sons.

And they took them wives of the women of Moab; the name of the one was Orpah, and the name of the other Ruth: and they dwelled there about ten years.

And Mahlon and Chilion died also both of them; and the woman was left of her two sons and her husband.

*Then she arose with her daughters in law, that she might return from the country of Moab: for **she had heard** in the country of Moab how that **the Lord had visited His people in giving them bread*** (Ruth 1:1-6).

People Leave the House of Bread for One Reason

Naomi and her husband and two sons left home and moved to Moab *because there was a famine in Bethlehem*. Consider the literal meaning of the Hebrew name of their hometown: Bethlehem means "house of bread." The reason they left the *house of bread* is that there was *no bread in the house*. It's simple, why people leave churches—there's no bread. Bread was part of the temple practices as well; it was proof of His presence—the *showbread*, the bread of the presence. Bread has always been the one thing historically that was an indicator of His presence. We find in the Old Testament that bread in the form of the showbread was in the Holy Place. It was called "the bread of the Presence" (Num. 4:7 NRSV). Showbread might better be interpreted as "show up bread," or in the Hebraic terms, "face bread." It was a heavenly symbol of God Himself.

Naomi and her family have something in common with the people who leave or totally avoid our churches today—they left *"that"* place and went somewhere else to try to find bread. I can tell you why people are flocking to the bars, the clubs, and the psychics by the millions. They're just trying to get by; they are just trying to survive because the Church has failed them. They looked, or their parents and friends looked and reported, and the spiritual cupboard was bare. There was no presence in the pantry; just empty shelves and offices full of recipes for bread. But the oven was cold and dusty.

We have falsely advertised and hyped-up our claims that there is bread in our house. But when the hungry come, all they can do is scrounge through the carpet for a few crumbs of yesteryears' revivals. We talk grandly about where He has been and what He has done, but we can say very little about what He is doing among us today. That isn't God's fault; it is ours. We have only remnants of what used to be—a residue of the fading glory. And unfortunately, we keep the veil of secrecy over that fact, much in the same way Moses kept the veil over his face after the shine of "glory dust" faded.[2] We camouflage our emptiness like the priesthood in Jesus' day kept the veil in place with no ark of the covenant behind it.

No Bread in the "House of Bread"

God may have to "pierce" the veil of our flesh to reveal our (the Church's) inner emptiness also. It's a pride problem—we point with pride to where He has been (protecting the temple tradition) while we deny the obviously apparent "glory" of the Son of God. The religious spirits of Jesus' day didn't want the populace to realize that there was no glory behind their veil. Jesus' presence presented problems. Religious spirits must preserve where He's been at the expense of where He is!

But a man with an experience is never at the mercy of a man with only an argument. "All I know is I was blind but now I see!" (See John 9:25.) If we can lead people into the manifest presence of God, all false theological houses of cards will tumble down.

Yet we wonder why people hardly bow their heads when they come in our meetings and places of worship. "Where has the fear of God gone?" we cry like A.W. Tozer. People don't sense God's presence in our gatherings because it's just not there sufficiently enough to register on our gauges. This, in turn, creates another problem. When people get just a little touch of God mixed with a lot of something that is not God, it inoculates them against the real thing. Once they've been "inoculated" by a crumb of God's presence, then when we say, "God really is here"; they say, "No, I've been there, done that. I bought that T-shirt, and I didn't find Him; it really didn't work for me." The problem is that God was there all right, but not enough of Him! There was no experience of meeting Him at the Damascus road. There was no undeniable, overwhelming sense of His manifest presence.

People have come to the House of Bread time and again only to find there was simply *too much of man* and *too little of God* there. The Almighty One is out to restore the sense of His awesome manifest presence in our lives

53

and places of worship. Over and over we talk about the glory of God covering the earth, but how is it going to flow through the streets of our cities if it can't even flow down the aisles of our churches? It's got to start somewhere, and it's not going to start out "there." It must start in "here"! It must start at "the temple," as Ezekiel wrote. "...I saw water coming out from under the threshold of the temple..." (Ezek. 47:1 NIV).

If God's glory can't flow through the aisles of the church because of seducing spirits and manipulating men, then God will have to turn somewhere else as He did the day Jesus rode past "the house of bread" (temple) in Jerusalem on a donkey. If there is no bread in the house, then I don't blame the hungry for not going there! I wouldn't!

A Rumor of Bread Reaches Moab

*W*hen Bethlehem, the house of bread, is empty, people are forced to look elsewhere for the bread of life. The dilemma they face is that the world's alternatives can be deadly. As Naomi was to discover, Moab is a cruel place. Moab will steal your sons from you and bury them before their time. Moab will separate you from your spouse. Moab will rob the very vitality of life from you. In the end, all that Naomi had left were two daughters-in-law whom she had known only ten years. With nothing but a gloomy and disastrous future staring her in the face, she told them, "You might as well not hang around me either. I don't have any more sons to give you." But then she said, "I heard a rumor...."[3]

There is an information "grapevine" that winds its way through every community, hamlet, and city of the world. It winds its way all down our coasts, over every mountain range, and into every place where men and women dwell. It is the "grapevine of the hungry." If just one of them hears the rumor that there is bread back in the House of Bread, the news will flow like a surge of electricity through a power line at near the speed of light. The news of bread will leapfrog from one household to the other, from one place to another almost instantaneously. You won't have to worry about advertising on TV or promoting it in the usual ways of the world. The hungry will just hear. The news will break:

> "No, it's not a fake! It's hard to believe, but *this time* it's not hype or manipulation. No, it's not just a trickle; it's not just crumbs in the carpet. *There really is bread back in the House of Bread!* God is in the Church!"

When that happens, we won't be able to hold them in our buildings, no matter how many services we conduct each day. Why? How? *All you must do is get the bread back!*

Contented With Crumbs in the Carpet

There is much more of God available than we have ever known or imagined, but we have become so satisfied with where we are and what we have that we don't *press in* for God's best. Yes, God is moving among us and working in our lives, but we have been content to comb the carpet for crumbs as opposed to having the abundant loaves of hot bread God has prepared for us in the ovens of Heaven! He has prepared a great table of His presence in this day, and He is calling to the Church, "Come and dine."

We ignore God's summons while carefully counting our stale crumbs of yesteryear's bread. Meanwhile millions of people outside our church walls are starving for life. They are sick and overstuffed with our man-made programs for self-help and self-advancement. They are starving for *Him,* not stories *about* Him. They want the food, but all we have to give them is a tattered menu vacuum-sealed in plastic to protect the fading images of what once was from the grasping fingers of the desperately hungry. This is why we see highly educated men and women wearing crystals around their necks in the hopes of getting in touch with something beyond themselves and their sad existence. Wealthy and poor alike flock to flashy seminars about enlightenment and inner peace, gullibly swallowing every bit of the unbelievable junk being passed off as the latest bright revelation from the other world.

How can this be? It should convict and shame the Church to see so many hurting and searching people turn to psychics, astrology, and spiritists for guidance and hope in their lives! People are so hungry that they are pouring millions of dollars into an overnight industry of the occult manned by fake soothsayers (even the genuine "mediums" or "channelers" who tap the dark world of the occult and satanic familiar spirits are rare among this bunch). They are so desperate for hope that they will accept canned script from paid marketers as spiritual insight. *Oh, the depth of spiritual hunger in the world!* There is only one reason so many people are so willing to attempt to get in touch with something from the other side, even accepting the counterfeit—they don't know where to find the real thing. The blame for that can only fall in one place. This hour seems to be custom-tailored for the Church of His presence to prevail.

Now I must repeat one of the shocking statements that I keep hearing God say in my spirit:

> *...there is as much of God in most bars*
> *as there is in most churches.*

It is no wonder that neither sinners nor saints feel the need to bow when they come into a worship service. They don't sense the presence of anything or anyone worthy of worship among us.

On the other hand, if the Church would become what it should and could become, then we'd have to scramble just to accommodate the demand for "bread" in the house. And when people would enter our houses of bread, no one would have to tell them to "bow their heads in prayer." They would fall on their faces before our holy God without a single word being spoken. Even the heathen would instinctively know that God Himself had entered the house.[4]

We would ask one another, "Who will man the phones tomorrow?" knowing the lines would be jammed with people calling in to say, "I've got to hear from God!" Why do I say this? Because when people pay the exorbitant price to psychics, they are really trying to touch God and find relief from the pain in their lives. They just don't know where else to go. King Saul gave us the example of the desperate wanderer cut off from God. When he couldn't reach or catch God, he said, "Then let me find a witch. Anybody! I've got to have a word if I have to disguise myself and sneak in the back door. I must have access to the spirit realm."[5]

There is another problem God is concerned with, and Jesus revealed it when He rebuked the religious leaders of His day: "Woe to you, teachers of the law and Pharisees, you hypocrites! You shut the kingdom of heaven in men's faces. You yourselves do not enter, nor will you let those enter who are trying to" (Mt. 23:13 NIV). It is bad enough when you refuse to go in yourself, but God gets extra agitated when you stand at the door and refuse to let anybody else in either! Through our ignorance of spiritual matters and our lack of hunger, we have figuratively "stood at the door" by the way we have done things, and have barred the lost and hungry from entering in. Our constant claims of hot bread backed only by stale crumbs on a frayed carpet of man's tradition have left countless generations hungry, homeless, and with nowhere else to go but Moab. And so they grow weary with the cruel taskmaster who takes his tax in their marriages, children, and lives.

Now, today, there is a faint rumor that there is bread in God's house once again. This generation, like Ruth (a picture of the unchurched unsaved), is about to sidle up to Naomi (a picture of a prodigal) to say, "If you heard there is really bread there, then I'm going with you. Wherever you go, I'll go. Your people will be my people, and your God will be my God" (see Ruth 1:16). *If*...there's really bread. So tattered was the reputation of Bethlehem (the house of bread) that Orpah didn't go. How many like her "don't go" because the history of hype from the Church exhausts their energy? They can't make the trip.

Do you know what will instantly integrate someone directly into the fabric of the local church? It will happen the moment they taste *the bread of His presence* in that place. When Ruth heard that there was bread back in Bethlehem, she rose from her sorrow to go to the house of bread.

Whatever Happened to the Bread?

The sign is still up. We still take people into our churches and show them the ovens where we used to bake bread. The ovens are all still in place and everything is there, but all you can find is crumbs from last year's visitation, and from the last great wave of revival our predecessors talked about. Now we are reduced to being shallow students of what we hope to experience some day. I'm constantly reading about revival, and God impressed upon me recently, "Son, you're reading about it because *you don't yet have the experience to write about.*"

I am tired of reading about God's visitations of yesteryear. I want God to break out somewhere in my lifetime so that in the future my children can say, *"I was there. I know; it's true."* God has no grandchildren. Each generation must experience His presence. Recitation was never meant to take the place of visitation.

By-products of Bread in the House

Two things happen when the bread of God's presence is restored to the Church. Naomi was a prodigal who left the house of bread when that table became bare. Yet once she heard that God had restored bread to Bethlehem, the house of bread, she quickly returned. *The prodigals will come walking back into Bethlehem* from Moab once they know there is bread in the house, and *they won't come alone.* Naomi came back to the house of bread accompanied by Ruth, who had never been there before. The never saved will come. As a result, Ruth became part of the Messianic lineage of Jesus when she married Boaz and bore him a son named Obed, who was the father of Jesse, the father of David.[6] Future royalty awaits our hunger-spurred actions.

Revival as we know it *"now"* is really the "recycling" of saved people through the Church to keep them fired up. But the next wave of true revival will bring waves of unchurched people into the House of Bread—people who have never darkened the door of a church in their lives. When they hear that there really is bread in the house, they will stream through our doors after smelling the fragrance of hot bread from the ovens of Heaven!

Often we are so full and satisfied with other things that we insist on "getting by" with our crumbs of the past. We're happy with our music the way it is. We're happy with our "renewal" meetings. It is time for some of what I have politely termed "divine discontent." Can I say it and not be judged? *I'm not happy.* By that I mean that even though I have been a participant in what some would call the revival of a lifetime, I am still not happy. Why? Because I know what *can* happen. I can catch Him. I know that there is far more than anything we have seen or hoped for yet, and it has become a holy obsession. I want God. I want more of Him.

The Key Seems to Be Less of Me

atan's ploy has been to keep us so full of junk that we're not hungry for Him, and it has worked magnificently for centuries. The enemy has made us so accustomed to surviving on an earthly prosperity but a beggar's subsistence in the spirit realm, that just a crumb of God's presence will satisfy. There are those who are not content with crumbs anymore. They want *Him* and nothing else will do. A full loaf! Counterfeits no longer satisfy or interest them; they must have the *real thing*. Most of us, however, keep our lives so jammed with junk food for the soul and amusements for the flesh that we don't know what it is to be really hungry.

Have you ever seen hungry people? I mean *really hungry* people. If you could come with me on a ministry trip to Ethiopia or travel to some famine-ravaged land, you would see what happens when sacks of rice are brought out among *really hungry* people. They come from everywhere in a matter of seconds. Most of us eat before we go to a church meeting, so the sight of a loaf of bread on a church altar wouldn't do anything for us. But when God told me one morning to preach about the bread, He also said "Son, if they were physically starving, *they would act differently.*" (Interestingly, an intercessor felt impressed to bake bread that morning and the pastor felt led to place it on the altar!) There was birthed that day a Heaven-induced hunger for the bread of His presence. That bread has provoked healing, restoration, and hunger for revival around the world.

The Bible says of the Kingdom of Heaven, "...the violent take it by force" (Mt. 11:12). For some reason that doesn't sound like us, does it? We've become so "churchified" that we have our own form of "political correctness" and polite etiquette. Since we don't want to be too radical, we line all the chairs up in nice rows and expect our services to conform to equally straight and regimented lines as well. We need to get so desperately hungry for Him *that we literally forget our manners*! The most apparent difference between liturgical worship and "charismatic" worship is that one has a printed program and the other is memorized. Often the one will even know when "God" will speak prophetically!

Everybody whom I can think of in the New Testament record who "forgot their manners" received something from Him. I'm not talking about rudeness for the sake of rudeness; I'm talking about rudeness born out of desperation! What about the desperate woman with an incurable hemorrhaging problem who elbowed and shoved her way through the crowd until she touched the hem of the Lord's garment?[7] What about the impertinent Canaanite woman who just kept begging Jesus to deliver her daughter from demonization in Matthew 15:22-28? Even though Jesus insulted her when He said, "It is not meet to take the children's bread, and to cast it to dogs" (Mt. 15:26b), she persisted. And she was so rude, so abrupt, and so pushy (or was she simply so *desperately hungry* for bread) that she replied, "Truth, Lord: yet the dogs eat of the crumbs which fall from their masters' table" (Mt. 15:27).

Most of us, on the other hand, come to our ministers and say, "Oh Pastor, would you, could you, pray for me and bless me?" If nothing really happens, we just shrug our shoulders and say, "Well, I'll go eat or I'll go relax," or "I'm going to go home and placate the inner man with fleshly food and entertainment."

To be honest, I'm hoping that God grips men and women in His Church and causes them to become so obsessed with the bread of His presence that they will not stop. Once that happens, they don't want just a "bless me" touch. They will want Him to show up in the place no matter how much it costs or how uncomfortable it may feel. They may sound and act rude, but they won't really care about man's opinion, only about God's opinion. It is accurate to say that the Church, by and large, doesn't really have a place for people like that.

One of the first steps to real revival is to recognize that you are in a state of decline. This isn't an easy task in our professed prosperity, but we need to say, "We're in decline; we're not in the best of times." Ironically, we find ourselves in the odd situation of matching the famous line from *A Tale of Two Cities* by Charles Dickens, "It was the best of times, it was the worst of times."[8]

It might be the best of times economically, but on the whole, the Church is not riding a wave of spiritual prosperity. How long has it been since your shadow healed anybody? How long has it been since your mere presence in a room caused people to say, "I've got to get right with God"? Where are the future Finneys and Wigglesworths? This happened with them.

I know a pastor in Ethiopia who was ministering in a service when men from the Communist government there interrupted the church service and said, "We are here to stop you from having church." They had already done everything they knew to do but without success, so that day they grabbed the pastor's three-year-old daughter and literally threw her out the second-story window of the building while everybody watched. The Communists thought that would stop the service, but the pastor's wife went down to the ground floor, cradled her dead baby in her arms, and returned to her seat on the front row and worship continued. As a result of this humble pastor's faithfulness, 400,000 devout believers would boldly show up for his Bible conferences in Ethiopia.

One time my father, a national leader in a Pentecostal denomination in America, was talking with this pastor. He knew that this pastor lived in horrible poverty in Ethiopia, and he made the mistake of showing a little bit of what he thought would be gracious sympathy. He told this Ethiopian pastor, "Brother, we pray for you in your poverty."

This humble man turned to my father and said, "No, you don't understand. *We pray for you in your prosperity.*" That took my father aback, but the Ethiopian pastor explained, "We pray for you Americans because it is much harder for you to live at the place God wants you to live in the midst of prosperity, than it is for us in the midst of our poverty."

The greatest trick the enemy has used to rob the American Church of its vitality has been the "lollipop of prosperity." I am not against prosperity. Be as prosperous as you want to be, but pursue Him instead of the prosperity. You see, it is very easy to begin chasing God and wind up chasing something else![9] Don't be like that. Be a God chaser. Period.

What If God *Really* Showed Up in Your Church?

If God really shows His "face" in your church, I can assure you that the "grapevine of the hungry" in your city or region will spread the news overnight!

Before you can even pry the doors open the next day, the hungry will come and stand in line for fresh bread. Why don't we see that kind of response now? The hungry have been "burned." As soon as the tiniest trickle of God's presence flows through our services, we want to tell the whole world, "There's a river of God's anointing that has broken out over here."

Unfortunately, most of the times we shout, "God is here!" the hungry come only to find that we have hyped and manipulated, and over-promoted and under-produced our goods. We've falsely portrayed every trickle of God's anointing as a mighty river, and to their dismay the only river they have found among us is a river of words. We sometimes even build magnificent bridges over dry riverbeds!

We can't expect the lost and the hurting to come running to our "river" only to discover that there's barely enough for them to get a single sip from God's glass. We've told them, "God is really here; there's food on the table," but every time they have believed our report, they have been forced to comb through the carpet for the mere crumbs of the promised feast. *Our past is more powerful than our present.*

Ye Have Not Because...

Compared to what God *wants to do*, we're digging for crumbs in the carpet when He has hot loaves baking in the ovens of Heaven! He is not the God of crumbs and lack. He is waiting just to dispense unending loaves of His life-giving presence, but our problem was described long ago by James the apostle, "...ye have not, because ye ask not" (Jas. 4:2b). Yet the psalmist David sings through the tunnel of time that "his seed" never go "begging for bread" (see Ps. 37:25).

We need to understand that what we have, where we are, and what we are doing is *small* compared to what He wants to do among and through us. Young Samuel was a prophet in a generation of transition much like ours. The Bible tells us that early in Samuel's life, "...the word of the Lord was precious in those days; there was no open vision" (1 Sam. 3:1).

One night Eli the old high priest went to bed, and by that point in his life his eyesight had grown so poor that he could barely see anything. Part of our problem in the historical Church is that our eyesight has grown dim and we can't see like we should. We've become satisfied with church proceeding in the dim "normal and status quo" mode. We just keep going through the motions, lighting the lamps and shuffling from dusty room to dusty room as if God was still speaking to us. But when He really does speak, we think people are dreaming. When He really does appear, dim eyes can't see Him. When He really does move, we are reluctant to accept it for fear we will "bump into something unfamiliar" in our dim, lamp-less darkness. It frustrates us when God "moves the furniture" on us. We tell the young Samuels among us, "Go back to sleep. Just keep doing things the way I've taught you to do them, Samuel. It's okay. It has always been this way."

No, it hasn't always been that way! And I'm not happy with it being that way—*I want more*! I don't know about you, but every empty seat I see in a church building screams out to me, "I could be filled with some former citizen of Moab! Can't you put a body in this seat?" I don't know about you, but that just feeds my holy frustration, my divine discontent.

> And [before] **the lamp of God went out in the temple of the Lord, where the ark of God was, and Samuel was laid down to sleep;**

That the Lord called Samuel: and he answered, Here am I (1 Samuel 3:3-4).

The lamp of God was flickering low and was just about to go out, but that didn't disturb Eli. (He lived in a permanent state of semi-darkness.) Young Samuel, though, said, "I hear something." It is time for us to admit that the lamp of God is flickering. Yes, it is still burning, but things are not as they should be. We look at this little flickering lamp casting low light in the Church here and there and say, "Oh, it's revival!" It may be for the handful who can get close enough to see it, but what about those who are at a distance? What about the lost who never read our magazines, watch our TV shows, or listen to the latest Christian teaching tapes? We need the light of the glory of God bright enough to be seen from a distance. In other words, it is time for the glory of God, the lamp of God, to break out of the Church "bushel" to illuminate our cities![10]

I believe that God is about to release the "spirit of a breaker" (see Mic. 2:13) to come and literally break the heavens open so that everybody can eat and feed at God's table. Before the heavens can open, though, the fountains of the deep must be broken.[11] It's time for some church, somewhere, to forget about trying to be a "politically correct church" and break open the heavens that the manna might fall and start feeding the spiritually hungry of the city! It's time that we punch a hole in the heavens and break through in hungry travail so the glory of God can begin to shine down on our city. But we can't even get a trickle to flow down the aisle, much less see His glory flow through the streets, *because we're not really hungry.* We are like the Laodiceans, full and content.

Father, I pray that a spirit of spiritual violence will grip our hearts, that You will turn us into warriors of worship. I pray that we will not stop until we break through the heavens, until there's a crack in the heavenlies, until there is an open heaven. Our cities and nation need You, Lord. We need You. We're tired of digging through the carpet for crumbs. Send us Your hot bread from Heaven, send us the manna of Your presence....

No matter what you need or feel you lack in your life—what you *really* need is *Him.* And the way to get Him is to get hungry. I pray that God will give you an impartation of *hunger* because that will qualify you for the promise of the fullness. Jesus said: "Blessed are they which do hunger and thirst after righteousness: for they shall be filled" (Mt. 5:6).

If we can get hungry, then He can make us holy. Then He can put the pieces of our broken lives back together. But our hunger is the key. So when you find yourself digging for crumbs in the carpet at the House of Bread, you should be praying, "Lord, stir up a firestorm of hunger in me."

☙ Notes from those on the chase ☙

*Y*our book, **The God Chasers**, has so revolutionized my
life. I have wanted more of God. It was about time that
I got a new pair of running shoes, though. I needed them if
I was going to start chasing God.

I had a dream of being a mouthpiece (or P.A. system) for
God on the streets of my city and in the bars. I wrote the
dream down in my journal and had not shared it with
anyone until I read your book and you talked about going
into the bars. Jesus would be in the bars where the sinners
are. He ate with sinners, tax collectors, and publicans. He
went where the hurting people were. I was getting uncomfortable just sitting in the pew and getting fed. After reading
your book, I can no longer keep quiet. I can no longer just
sit in the pew and do nothing. God is calling me to go out
into the byways. I have heard the "trumpet call." I have become a "God Chaser" and a people chaser. I am going fishing, and I am going to catch some people for God. They, in
turn, are going to become "God Chasers," and they will, in
turn, catch more people for God who will become "God
Chasers." Praise God! I am still chasing hard after Him.

—Carla S.

☙   ☙

I am sure that there are countless others who have experienced a life-changing revelation in worship by reading
your book, **The God Chasers**.

My husband and I have been pastoring our small church for
the past eight years now and felt that there has to be more
to coming to the church day in and day out. We were both
starving for the presence of God as we had never known. As
pastors, we feel that we are the example before our people,
and if we aren't presenting it, they aren't getting it! One of

the men in our church gave me a copy of your book, and I HATE to read! I opened the first page to read and found that it fed life to my soul. Tears fell like rain as I read about going to the bakery for bread and finding no bread. Going to the house for bread and finding no bread. Our church has been bound by the motions of coming to church. I not only read your book, but I have started teaching from it with the study guide. My husband is preaching as never before. We come to church as though no one else is here because no one else matters to us as we enter the house of the Lord. We come with anticipation of HIS presence and HIS anointing. The people caught up with traditions have left, and we are blessing them coming in and blessing them going out. Our congregation is getting on fire and a new life is being birthed in our church because we are not here for man's purpose, but we are here for HIS purpose. I pray God's continued anointing in your ministry as well as on your penning to paper what HE reveals to you by HIS Spirit. Thank you for allowing God's presence to flow through you!

—Debra M.

❧   ❧

*I read The God Chasers about two and a half years ago in the spring of '99 after my son and I had attended our first crusade by Benny Hinn Ministries in Detroit ('98). My son was attending a Bible college and asked one day, "Mom, have you read **The God Chasers** yet?" I replied that I hadn't and didn't even know who Tommy Tenney was. "Why should I read it?" I inquired.*

"Because, Mom, when you do, God shows up!" So, he brought me a copy of the book to read.

I don't remember what exactly that I read impacted me the most, but I do know that there was a stirring in my heart beyond any other author I had ever read, and before I had finished the first chapter, I had to put the book down because I was sobbing so hard.

I have been a born-again believer for more than 20 years. It is the presence of God that has revolutionized my life with Him...first at the Benny Hinn crusade and then with Tommy's books.

My most favorite book of all time is **God's Favorite House**. *I have read and reread it so much that it is falling apart. I just bought a copy for my pastor as it was while reading this book for the second or third time and praying to be in a church where God is welcome in His own house that the Holy Spirit directed me to meet my pastor and his wife in our local post office. After attending church there for the first time, the Holy Spirit spoke on my way home. "Crista, now you don't have to eat the crumbs anymore. Now you may come to the banquet table."*

The change in my personal and corporate worship time is beyond what I have time or space to tell you.

—Crista H.

Ask Some Questions

1. What do you think it would look like if God were to "show up" in your city or town? Do people see that God has "shown up" in your life? *Today*, how can you let God "show up"?

2. Many people mistake inner hunger for the need of some kind of natural satisfaction. The emptiness we feel inside should drive us closer to the only One who can truly satisfy. When your soul is hungry, what do you tend to fill it up with?

3. Page 27 speaks about people who are starving in countries like Ethiopia. What would your church service look like if people got that hungry for God?

4. Are you hungry for more of God? *Be happy!* Jesus said in Matthew 5:6 that you are blessed—happy and to be envied—if you are hungry! He loves to satisfy the hungry heart with His presence. Are you hungry for a deeper relationship with Him? How is that hunger evident in your daily life?

Endnotes

1. Bethlehemjudah is the full name of the city, much like Atlanta, Georgia. Judah refers to the land of the tribe of Judah.

2. See 2 Cor. 3:13 NIV.

3. See Ruth 1:6.

4. See 1 Cor. 14:25 NAS.

5. See 1 Sam. 28:7.

6. See Ruth 4:17.

7. See Mt. 9:20-22.

8. Charles Dickens, *A Tale of Two Cities, Book I,* Chapter 1.

9. By "chasing God," I am referring to our pursuit of Him as our chief aim and very reason for being—after salvation. I am not implying that we are saved by our works. Salvation is a work of grace alone through the finished work of Christ Jesus on the cross and His resurrection from the dead. Although this will be obvious to most readers, I thought it wise to include this important statement for those who may wonder.... I highly recommend A.W. Tozer's book, *The Pursuit of God.*

10. See Mt. 5:15.

11. See Gen. 1:8; 7:11.

Chapter 3

THERE'S GOT TO BE MORE

Rediscovering the manifest presence of God

I don't know about you, my friend, but there's a driving passion in my heart that whispers to me that there's more than what I already know, more than what I already have. It makes me jealous of John, who wrote Revelation. It makes me envious of people who get glimpses out of this world into that world and see things that I only dream about. I know there's more. One reason I know there's more is because of those who have encountered the "more" and were never the same. God chasers! My prayer is, *I want to see You like John saw You!*

In all my reading and study of the Bible, I have never found any person mentioned in the Scriptures who really had a "God encounter" and then "backslid" and rebelled against God. Once you experience God in His glory, you can't turn away from Him or forget His touch. It's not just an argument or a doctrine; it's an *experience.* That is why the apostle Paul said, "...I know *whom* I have believed..." (2 Tim. 1:12). Unfortunately, many people in the Church would say, "I know about *whom* I have believed." That means they haven't met Him in His glory.

One reason people flow *out* the back doors of our churches as fast as they come in through the front door is because they have more of a "man encounter" with our programs than a "God encounter" with the unforgettable majesty and power of the Almighty God. What is needed are "Damascus road experiences" like Saul's encounter with God Himself.[1]

This speaks strongly of the difference between the *omnipresence* of God and the *manifest presence* of God. The phrase, "omnipresence of God," refers to the fact that He is everywhere all the time. He is that "particle" in the atomic nucleus that nuclear physicists cannot see and can only track. The Gospel of John touches on this quality of God when it says, "And without Him was not any thing made that was made" (Jn. 1:3b). God is everywhere in everything. He is the composite of everything, both the glue that holds the pieces of the universe together and the pieces themselves! This explains why people can sit on a bar stool in an inebriated state and suddenly feel the conviction of the Holy Spirit without the benefit of a preacher, gospel music, or any other Christian influence. God is literally right there in the bar with them, and the mind-numbing ability of alcohol to lower inhibitions also allows them to lose their inhibitions toward God. Unfortunately by then it is not always a "choice" of their will that moves them toward God, just the hunger of their hearts. Their "mind" is numb; their heart is hungry. When their "mind" recovers to discover the will is unbroken, they often revert because it was not a valid encounter. A hungry heart inside a man with an unbowed head (mind) and an unbroken (unsubmitted) will is a recipe for misery.

Now if God can do that in the bar room, why should we be surprised at all the other things He can do "all by Himself"? (Most people who don't come from a church background will tell you that the first time they felt the prick of the conviction of God was in some place *other* than in a church service or religious setting.) All these instances illustrate the effects of the omnipresence of God, the quality of His presence being everywhere, all the time.

The *Manifest* Presence of God

*Y*et even though God is everywhere all the time, there are also times when He *concentrates* the very essence of His being into what many call "the manifest presence of God." When this happens, there is a strong sense and awareness that God Himself has "entered the room." You might say that although He is indeed everywhere all the time, there are also specific periods of time when He is "here" *more* than "there." For divine reasons, God chooses to concentrate or reveal Himself more strongly in one place than another, or more at one time than another.

This concept may disturb you theologically. You may be thinking, *Wait a minute. God is always here. He's omnipresent.* That's true, but why did He say, "If My people, which are called by My name, shall humble themselves, and pray, and seek My *face*...."? (2 Chron. 7:14.) If they are already His people, what other level of "Him" are they to "seek"? Seek His face! Why? It is because His *favor* flows wherever His *face* is directed. You can be God's child and not have His favor, much as an earthly child would be in disfavor but not be disowned. That phrase in the verse is particularly interesting. God told His people for all generations that if they would seek His face and "turn from their wicked ways," then He would hear them and heal

75

their land. How can we be God's people and have wicked ways? Perhaps our "wicked ways" explain why we have been content just to be in God's vicinity instead of gazing upon His face. The only thing that is going to turn the focus and favor of God toward us is our hunger. We must repent, reach for His face, and pray, "God, look at us, and we'll look to You."

Guided By the Eye of God

Too often God's people can be guided only by the written Word or the prophetic word. The Bible says He wants us to move beyond that to a place marked by a greater degree of tenderness of heart toward Him and by a deeper maturity that allows Him to "guide us with His eye" (see Ps. 32:8-9). In the kind of home in which I was raised, my mom or dad could just look at me a certain way and get the job done. If I was straying down the path of childhood foolishness, they didn't always have to say anything. Just the look in their eyes as they glanced or glared toward me would give me the guidance that I needed. Do you still *need* to hear a thundering voice from behind the pulpit? A biting prophetic utterance to correct your ways? Or are you able to read the emotion of God on His face? Are you tenderhearted enough that His eye can guide you and convict your heart of sin? When He glances your way, are you quick to say, "Oh, I can't do that. I can't go there, and I can't say that because it would displease my Father"? The glance of God convicted Peter, and to the altar music of a rooster crowing he wept his way to tenderness.

God is everywhere, but *He doesn't turn His face and His favor everywhere*. That is why He tells us to seek His face. Yes, He is present with you every time you meet with other believers in a worship service, but how long has it been since your hunger caused you to crawl up in His lap, and like a child, to reach up and take the face of God to turn it toward you? Intimacy with Him! That is what God desires, and His face should be our highest focus.

The Israelites referred to the manifest presence of God as the *shekinah* glory of God. When David began to talk about bringing the ark of the covenant back to Jerusalem, he wasn't interested in the gold-covered box with the artifacts inside it. He was interested in the blue flame that hovered between the outstretched wings of the cherubim on top of the ark. That is what he wanted, because there was something about the flame that signified that God Himself was present. And wherever that glory or manifested presence of God went, there was victory, power, and blessing. Intimacy will bring about "blessing," but the pursuit of "blessing" won't always bring about intimacy.

What we cry for is a restoration of the manifested presence of God. When Moses was exposed to the glory of God, the residue of that glory caused his face to shine so much that when he came back down from the mountain, the people said, "Moses, you must cover your face. We can't bear to look at you" (see Ex. 34:29-35). Whatever or whoever is exposed to the manifested presence of God begins to absorb the very material matter of God. Can you imagine what it was like in the Holy of Holies? How much of the glory of God had been absorbed by those badger skins, the veil, and the ark itself?

The Legacy of a Place Where God Lingers

When God begins to visit in a place or among a people, unusual things start happening simply because He is there. If you don't believe me, ask Jacob. Look particularly at his flight from his problems. At one point, God told him to go back to Bethel, meaning "house of God," and Jacob essentially told his family

77

members, "*If we can just get back to Bethel*, I'll build an altar to God and we'll be all right" (see Gen. 35:1-3). He knew there was a lingering presence of God at Bethel.

It is interesting to read what happened when Jacob and his family made that trip to Bethel: "And they journeyed: and *the terror of God* was upon the cities that were round about them, and they did not pursue after the sons of Jacob" (Gen. 35:5). The Hebrew word for "terror" comes from a root word that means "to prostrate; hence to break down, either by violence, or by confusion and *fear*."[2] If we want the "fear of the Lord" to return to the world, then the Church must return to Bethel, the place of His manifest presence.

Stumbling Into the Cloud

The manifest presence of God often lingers in a place even when no one else is around. I remember the day a member of the church staff at a church that God invaded crossed the platform in the sanctuary on a weekday to refresh the platform water. He never made it back. Three hours later somebody noticed that he was gone and they went looking for him. The light was dim in the sanctuary, and when they turned on the lights, they saw the man lying prostrate on the platform where he had fallen after stumbling into the cloud of His presence.

There have been times when a cloud of the presence of God would suddenly show up as God's people worshiped. Now that is when things get scary. It could be the mist of the glory of God beginning to congeal itself before our eyes. I don't understand it; I'm just telling you it has happened.

One of the pastors there had a brother-in-law who was an atheist. In fact, he wasn't just an atheist; he was an "evangelistic atheist." This brother-in-law was the kind of guy whom you wanted to avoid at family gatherings because he always caused trouble and started heated arguments. In the middle of God's invasion of this particular church, this brother-in-law called the pastor's wife (who was his sister). He told her, "Look, I'm flying in. Would you pick me up? I just want to spend a couple of days with you."

The pastor knew something was up, because this brother-in-law had never done that before. When he arrived, it was obvious that he didn't know what he was doing there. It was the strangest thing. There they were, trying to make conversation with each other when they had nothing in common. They talked about the weather, and then they ran into one of those awkward long silences in the car coming back from the airport. As they passed by the church, the pastor said, "That's the church. We just finished some remodeling."

Since the brother-in-law had never seen it, and figuring it was yet another way to plug an awkward moment of silence, this pastor said, "You wouldn't want to go in and look at it, would you?"

To his complete surprise, his atheist brother-in-law said, "Yes, I would."

"I'm Not Ready for This!"

The pastor pulled into the church parking lot and then unlocked the door to the church building. His brother-in-law was right behind him, and the pastor's wife was third in line. The pastor stepped inside and held the door open for his brother-in-law, and the moment the man's foot touched the floor on the other side of the threshold, he crumpled in a heap and began to weep and cry out, "My God, help me! I'm not ready for this. I don't know how to do this! What am I going to do?"

Then he grabbed the pastor and said, "Tell me how to get saved *right now*!" The whole time he was writhing on the floor and crying uncontrollably. So this pastor led his brother-in-law to the Lord right there while he was sprawled half-in and half-out of the building while his sister patiently held the door open! Her atheist brother had an encounter with the "residue" or lingering presence of the glory of God.

As soon as he regained a measure of coherence, they asked him, "What happened to you?" He said, "I don't know how to explain it. All I know is that when I was outside the building I was an atheist and I didn't believe that God existed. But when I stepped across that threshold, *I met Him* and I knew it was God. I knew *I had to get right*, and I felt horrible about my life." Then he added, "It just took all the strength out of me."

What could happen in a city or a region if this strength of "presence" expanded beyond the localized area of the church building?

The Anointing and the Glory

 hen the anointing of God rests on human flesh, it makes everything flow better. One of the clearest pictures of the anointing and its purpose in the Bible is provided in the Book of Esther. When Esther was being prepared for her presentation to the king of Persia, she was required to go through a year of purification during which she was repeatedly soaked in fragrant anointing oil (ironically using virtually the same ingredients of the Hebrews' worship incense and anointing oil). *One year in preparation for one night with the king!* A logical side benefit of all those soaking baths in perfumed oil is that every man who came near to Esther would think or say, "My, but you smell good." Nevertheless, Esther wouldn't give them the time of day for the same reason that you and I should never be distracted by the pursuit of man's approval:

The purpose of the anointing is not to make man like you, but to make the king like you.

It is far more important that the King approve of you than the people. David was anointed by God long before he was crowned by the people. He sought God's approval over man's—he was a God chaser!

We have prostituted God's anointing too many times. We prepare for Him and we soak in His precious, sweet-smelling anointing, but then all we do is parade it around for man! We end up flirting on the way to the chamber of the king and never make it, seduced by other, lower lovers. We need to remember that our King is not going to have "soiled goods." Only the virgins are fit to go in to the King. I'm saying that we prostitute the anointing in the sense that we say, "That was good preaching!" or "That song was really good!" and we give man the glory and the attention (or we seek man's glory and attention). We seek to please man (the flesh). Even our services are structured to please man. The anointing really does do a lot of wonderful things in our lives, and it breaks the yoke of oppression. But that is only a by-product. It is much like when I splash cologne on for my wife. The by-product is that I smell good to everyone. But the purpose of the perfume was for her, not them! The problem comes when we use it to impress and flirt with one another, overlooking the primary purpose of the anointing, which is to camouflage the stench of our own flesh.

When Esther entered the king's "house of women," she was given oils and soaps for purification and subjected to a soaking process designed to turn a peasant girl into a princess. Again, the real purpose of the anointing is not to make us sound good, look good, or smell good to man. That happens as a by-product, but the real purpose of the anointing is to give us favor in the king's chamber. Our flesh stinks to God and the anointing makes us acceptable to the King. It's God's process of turning peasants into princesses—prospective brides-to-be!

The anointing may make us worship or preach better, but we need to remember that the anointing—whether it falls on us individually or on a congregation during a service—is not the end, but just the beginning. Some would prostitute the anointing by "dancing around in front of the veil" of God's presence, not realizing that its whole purpose is to prepare them to *enter in*, to go past the veil into His glory. The King's chamber, the Holy of Holies, awaits the anointed. The holy anointing oil was literally rubbed on and into everything in the Holy Place, *including the garments of the priest*. They then took "powdered perfume" to anoint the very atmosphere.

> *And he* [Aaron and his successors] *shall take a censer full of burning coals of fire from off the altar before the Lord, and his hands full of sweet incense beaten small, and bring it within the veil:*
> *And he shall put the incense upon the fire before the Lord, that the cloud of the incense may cover the mercy seat that is upon the testimony, that he die not* (Leviticus 16:12-13).

Under the ordinances of the Old Testament, the last thing the high priest did before he entered into the Holy of Holies was to place a handful of incense (symbolic of the anointing) into a censer and thrust his hands and the censer through the veil to make a dense screen of smoke. Why? To "...cover the mercy seat...that he die not" (Lev.

16:13b). The priest had to make enough smoke to camouflage or conceal his flesh from God's presence.

The anointing speaks of the action of man in worship. It was anointed worship that filled the Holy of Holies with smoke and made it possible for a man to stand in God's presence in a concealed place and live. At other times in the Old Testament, God stepped out of the Holy of Holies and made His own cloud of covering so mankind wouldn't see Him and perish. Under the old covenant based on the blood of bulls and goats, the priest of flesh had to make so much covering smoke that everything he did in the Holy of Holies had to be done by touch and not by sight. We walk by "faith," and not by sight! *God, I know You're in here somewhere.*

We Dance at the Veil and Refuse to Go In

*T*he Word of God tells us that the veil of division was torn in two by Jesus Christ's death on Calvary, and that we have free entry into God's presence through the blood of Jesus. We just aren't entering in. Occasionally somebody falls or stumbles his way past the veil during our dancing sessions and then comes back with a wild-eyed stare. But we usually go back into our dancing mode right in front of the veil. We get all excited about the possibility but we never really consummate the process. *The purpose of the anointing is to help us make the transition from flesh into glory.* One reason we like to linger in the anointing is that it makes the flesh feel good. On the other hand, when the glory of God comes, the flesh doesn't feel very comfortable.

When the glory of God comes, we become like the prophet Isaiah. Our flesh is so weakened by His presence that it is unnecessary for man to do anything other than behold Him in His glory. I've come to the conclusion that, in His presence, I am a man without a vocation. There's no need for me to preach if God shows up in His glory.[3] The people are already convinced of His holiness simply by His presence. Simultaneously, they are convicted of their un-holiness and their need to repent and live holy before Him. They are aware of His worthiness to receive praise and worship, and they are seized by a driving desire to dive deeper and lead others into His presence!

Jacob prayed and wrestled for a blessing, but what he received was a "changing." His name, his walk, and his demeanor were changed. I'm convinced that, in order to bring godly *change* into our lives, sometimes God puts a little spot of "death" in our bodies (as in Jacob's hip).[4] Something dies within us every time we are confronted by His glory. It's a "handle" for the holy. Just as Isaiah received the hot coals on his lips, we receive the hot bread of His presence and are forever changed. When more of our flesh dies, more of our spirit lives. The first six chapters of Isaiah's prophecy is devoted to "woe." He says, "Woe is me, woe is you, and woe is everybody." But after the prophet saw the Lord high and lifted up, he began to talk about things that can only be understood in the context of the New Testament.

One thing *hasn't changed*: the process of receiving the "blessing" of the hip, or the hot coal of God's glory on our lips of flesh, still doesn't feel good. It still makes us very uncomfortable as we dance around in front of the veil. The priests of old instinctively knew that God's glory wasn't something to trifle with. That is why they tied a rope around the high priest's ankle before he passed through the veil. They knew that if he entered God's presence in presumption or sin, then he wouldn't be walking out of there. They would have to drag his dead body back into our realm outside the veil and hope things would go better the next time. We must face some of the same issues today as we obey God's call for the Church to move from the anointing into His manifest glory.

"It Was Too Much of God"

*C*ertain people throughout Church history have known about the glory. Smith Wigglesworth was certainly one who knew about it. In one of the biographies about his life, the story is told that a pastor began to pray with Wigglesworth, and he was determined to stay in the prayer room with him. In the end, he finally had to crawl out of the room on his hands and knees, saying, "It was too much of God." That is possible. You can walk at that place. Ask Enoch. The end result of this quest is that all that remains is God's glory, not man's anointed gifts, ministry, opinions, or abilities. In God's manifest presence, you and I will need to do very little, yet great and mighty things will happen. On the other hand, when you and I do "our thing," the results are few and there isn't much of God's glory in it. That's the difference.

Another illustration of the difference between the anointing and the glory is this: When you scrape your feet across the carpet on a fresh cold day and touch the tip of someone's nose, you will get a spark. You will also get a spark if you grab a 220-volt power line with your bare hands. In both cases, the power behind the spark is electricity and they both operate from the same principle. One will just give you a spark, but the other has the potential to instantly kill you or to light up your whole world. They both share the same source, but they differ in power, purpose, and scope.

If we allow God to replace our programs with His manifested presence, then whenever people walk through the doors of our local church building or when they mingle with us at the mall, they will be convicted of sin and could rush to get right with God without a word being spoken. (we'll deal with this in more detail in Chapter 8, entitled "The Purpose of His Presence.")

We Do Not Have a Lock on God

We need to learn how to entertain and welcome the *manifested* presence of God to such a degree that just the residue of what has gone on among us brings sinners to the point of conviction and conversion instantaneously. I am hungry for that kind of expression of revival, but if we're not careful we are going to let the lamp flicker out. We do not have a lock on God because we're not married to Him yet. He is still just looking for a bride without spot or wrinkle, and we need to remember that He already left one bride at the altar and He'll leave another.

I believe that God will literally destroy the Church *as we know it* if He has to so He can reach the cities. He is not in love with our imperfect versions of His perfect Church; He is only out to claim the house that *God built*. If our foul-smelling, man-made monstrosity stands in the way of what He wants to do, then He will move our junk pile aside to reach the hungry. His heart is to reach the lost, and if He spared not His own Son to save the lost, then He won't spare us either.

We must move into agreement with what God wants to do. The same Bible you and I carry to church services week after week says, "If we don't praise Him, then the rocks will cry out."[5] If the Church won't praise Him and obey Him, then He will raise up people who will. If we won't sing of God's glory in the streets of the cities, then He will raise up a generation that is nonreligious and uninhibited and reveal His glory to them. His problem is that we suffer from the spiritually fatal disease of reluctance. We're just not hungry enough!

Only Repentance Will Get Us Anywhere

God is not coming to people who merely seek His benefits. He's coming to people who seek His face. In the Old Testament, when a person refused to show you his face, he was deliberately turning away from you. Ancient orders of the Church practiced "shunning." We can brag on our accomplishments or we can ignore our inadequacies, but no matter what we do, only repentance will get us anywhere with God.

The only way He will turn His visitation in revival into habitation for life is if you and I will prepare a place for Him with tears and repentance, because then He will no longer be found to wink at our ignorance. He will literally close His eyes and not look at us, lest His godly glance destroy us.

God is tired of screaming instructions at the Church; He wants to guide us with His eye. That means we have to be close enough to Him to see His face. He's tired of correcting us through public censure. We have sought His hands for too long. We want what He can do for us; we want His blessings, we want the chills and the thrills, we want the fishes and the loaves. Yet we shirk at the high commitment it takes to pursue His face.

If you seek His face, what you get is His favor. We have long enjoyed the omnipresence of God, but now we are experiencing brief moments of visitation by His manifest presence. It causes every hair to stand up on end, and it makes demonic forces flee and run.

When the anointing comes, if you're a preacher you preach better. But when the glory falls, you can't do anything. You stumble and stutter and just want to get out of the way. When you're a singer and you're anointed, you sing better. But when the glory falls, you can barely sing. Why? Because God declared that no flesh is going to glory in His presence.[6] This doesn't mean that you are a bad person or that you live in sin. It means that you are flesh and blood caught in the very presence of God. Doesn't this evoke longing memories of what happened at the dedication of Solomon's temple? The priest and minister couldn't stand to minister.[7] They weren't blasted back from blessing; I think they were fallen faceward from fear!

"If I've Ever Heard God—That Was God"

*W*hen the glory falls, people find themselves doing very odd things. I've seen it night after night during meetings in places of holy outbreak. One night a lady said, "I've never been to this church. Honestly, I was planning to leave my husband in the morning. But at 7:30 tonight [the services had started 30 minutes earlier at 7:00], I was sitting at my supper table when God spoke to me. If I've ever heard God, that was God. He said to me, 'Get up and go over to that church right now—the building with the green roof on it.' "

She came to the church building (with the green roof) and made it as far in as the back pews. Then she fell on her face between the back pews and wept in repentance for two hours. Nobody had to tell her what to do. Needless to say, her marriage was saved.

Real Revival Is When...

*W*e don't understand revival; in fact, we don't even have the slightest concept of what true revival is. For generations we have thought of revival in terms of a banner across the road or over a church entryway. We think revival means a silver-tongued preacher, some good music, and a few folks who decide they're going to join the church. No! Real revival is when people are eating at a restaurant or walking through the mall when they suddenly begin to weep and turn to their friends and say, "I don't know what's wrong with me, but I know I've got to get right with God."

Real revival is when the most "difficult" and unreachable person you know comes to Jesus against all odds and possibilities. Frankly, the main reason such people aren't reached any other time is because they are seeing too little of God and too much of man. We've tried to cram doctrine down people's throats, and we've printed enough tracts to paper the walls of entire buildings. I thank God for every person reached by a gospel tract, but people don't want doctrine, they don't want tracts, and they don't want our feeble arguments; they just want Him! (When will we learn that if people can be argued into the faith, then they can just as easily be argued out of it as well?) People may be attracted by our great music for a while, but it will only keep them interested as long as the music is good. We must not compete with the world in areas where they are as competent (or better than) us. They can't compete with God's presence.

I can tell you a secret right now if you promise *to* tell someone else. Do you want to know when people will start coming inside the confines of your local church building? They will come as soon as they hear that the *presence of God* is in the place. It's time to rediscover the power of the manifest presence of God.

God is looking for enough hungry people to receive His presence. When He comes, you won't need any advertisements in the newspaper, or on radio or television. All you need is God, and people will come from far and near on any given night! I'm not talking about theory or fiction—it is already happening. It all begins with the prayer of the hungry:

There's got to be more...

≋ Notes from those on the chase ≋

*Greetings in the name of the Lord. Thank you ever so much for the work you are doing in the Kingdom. I have just finished reading **The God Chasers** and **The God Catchers**. Both books were loaned to me by some friends. I have had a longing to know God like Moses did; these books have set my desire on fire. I have longed for passion in my relationship with the Lord, and these books have increased the depth and the width of this longing. They have helped to give me direction in my pursuit of God. I will not rest until I "catch" Him. Thank you for letting me know that it is possible. I now want to get my own copies of these books. May God continue to bless and establish your work.*

—Judith I.

≋ ≋

*It's indeed great to have read **The God Chasers** and **The God Catchers**...it has ignited a great fire within me that has changed my perception of God and set me alight for His presence!...Kudos to God for revealing His heart through you to so many others!*

—Luke P.

Ask Some Questions

1. What is the difference between the omnipresence of God and the manifest presence of God? Do you know (or know of) any modern day individuals who have had "Damascus Road" encounters with God? Have you ever had an encounter with God that forever changed you?

2. Who were some of God's favorite people in the Bible? Were they perfect? Why did God delight in them?

3. If we want God's manifest presence in our church services, what do we need to do? Where will it begin?

Endnotes

1. See Acts 9:3-6.

2. James Strong, *Strong's Exhaustive Concordance of the Bible* (Peabody, MA: Hendrickson Publishers, n.d.), **terror** (#H2847, #H2865).

3. See Heb. 8:11 NIV.

4. To this day some Jews will not eat meat from that corresponding place on an animal. See Gen. 32:32.

5. See Lk. 19:40.

6. See 1 Cor. 1:29.

7. See 1 Kings 8.

Chapter 4

DEAD MEN SEE HIS FACE

The secret path to His presence

" *I* know it's here somewhere; I can tell I'm close. There has got to be a way to get in there. Oh, there it is. This path doesn't look really nice, though. In fact, it's kind of broken and bloody. Let's see what they call this path... Repentance. Are you sure this is the way? Are you sure this is how I can reach my goal of His face and His presence? I'm going to ask a fellow traveler. Moses, what do you say? You've been there; tell me."

> *And the Lord said unto Moses, I will do this thing also that thou hast spoken: for thou hast found grace in My sight, and I know thee by name.*
> *And he said, I beseech Thee, show me Thy glory.*
> *And He said, Thou canst not see My face: for **there shall no man see Me, and live** (Exodus 33:17-18,20).*

When Moses asked God to show him His glory, the Lord warned him that no man can see Him and live. Even in the new covenant, this statement is true. Only dead men can see God. There is a connection between His glory and our death.

When Moses began to press the case with God and said, "I want to, I've got to," Moses already had the outline of the tabernacle. He was the man God chose to receive the architectural details of the pre-Calvary model of salvation and man's ultimate restoration to His presence. I am positive that Moses looked at the tabernacle and the law and thought, *This is not really it; this is just some sort of a model of what God is going to do. It's only a type, a shadow.* I think he knew that the furniture and utensils of the tabernacle all had symbolic meaning. He wanted to see the finished product. This man "started a cathedral" that was too big to build in one generation, so he said, "Show me Your glory." That was when the Lord said, "You can't. Only dead men can see My face."

That's why I love to read about the visionary prayers of people like Aimee Semple McPherson and William Seymour who used to stick his head in an apple crate during all-night prayer meetings on Azusa Street and pray for the glory of God to come down. I believe that when the conglomerate prayers of God's people gather together and finally reach a crescendo of power, hunger, and intensity, it finally gets to be "too much" for God to delay any longer. At that point He finally says, "That's it. I won't wait any longer. It is time!"

That is what happened in Argentina in the 1950s. A man named Edward Miller wrote a book entitled, *Cry for Me Argentina*, in which he describes one of the origins of the great revival in Argentina that was destined to impact South America and ultimately the entire world. Dr. Miller is now in his eighties, but more than four decades earlier he was one of but a few Pentecostal or Full Gospel missionaries working in Argentina. He tells the story of how

50 students in his Argentine Bible Institute began to pray and had an angelic visitation. They had to suspend classes because of the heavy prayer burden they had for the nation of Argentina. Day after day for 49 days in a row, these students prayed and interceded for Argentina in this Bible school. Argentina was a spiritual wasteland at the time, as far as Dr. Miller knew. He said he only knew of 600 Spirit-filled believers in the entire nation during those years under the government of Juan Peron.

Dr. Miller told me that he had never seen people weep so hard and so long in prayer. It had to be supernatural in origin and purpose. We don't know much about interceding today. Many of us think it consists of screaming against evil spirits, but that's not what needs to happen. We simply need for "Father" to show up.

It Could Only Be Described As "Unearthly Weeping"

Dr. Miller told me that those students wept and cried day after day. He mentioned that one young man leaned his head against a concrete brick wall and wept until, after four hours, a trail of tears had run down the porous wall. After six hours had passed, he was standing in a puddle of his own tears! These young intercessors wept day after day, and he said it could only be described as unearthly weeping. These students weren't simply repenting for something they had done. They had been moved by the Spirit into something called "vicarious repentance," in which they began to repent for what had happened through others in their city, their region, and in the country of Argentina.

Dr. Miller said that on the fiftieth day of continuous intercession and weeping before the Lord, a prophetic word came forth that declared, "Weep no more, for the

Lion of the tribe of Judah hath prevailed over the prince of Argentina." Eighteen months later, Argentines were flocking to evangelistic healing services in soccer stadiums that seated 180,000 people, and even the largest stadiums in the nation weren't big enough to contain the crowds.

I'll never forget what he told me:

> "If God can get enough people in an area to reject the rulership and the dominion of satan, if enough of His people will reject satan's dominion in the right way—with humility, with brokenness, and in repentant intercession, then God will slap an eviction notice on the doorway of the ruling demonic power of that area. And when He does, then there is a light and glory that begins to come."

We are really praying for an opening in the heavens over our cities and our nation so that when the glory of God comes, the people in our area can't resist anymore because the stronghold of demonic powers is broken. How does that happen? It happens through a visitation of the manifestation of the glory of God. Oh, that "prayers" would arise that would both close the gates of hell and open the windows of Heaven!

We Like to Dance Around Burning Bushes

*O*ne of our problems is that whenever we have good services or feel like revival has come, we tend to camp out at that spot and pull aside from our pursuit of God so we can dance around burning bushes. We get so caught up in what happened at the bush that we never go back to Egypt and set the people free!

God is telling His Church that it's not enough just to be blessed. It is not enough to receive His gifts and walk in

His anointing. I don't want more blessings; I want the Blesser. I don't want any more gifts; I want the Giver. "Are you saying you don't believe in gifts, that you don't want God's blessings?" No, I'm saying that sometimes in our emotional frenzy over seeing something from the "other world" briefly visit this world, we get overwhelmed and distracted from our divine purpose. Don't just get excited about the "toys" that God has; *He wants you to be excited about Him.*

My ministry requires me to travel quite often, and when I come home to my family, I don't get too excited when I am peppered with questions by my children: "What did you bring me, Daddy? Did you get me any-thing?" I realize that is normal for little children, but what I really want, what I dream about almost every day I am away, is the moment my six-year-old just crawls up in my lap and "loves" on me with no thoughts about what toy I've tucked into my suitcase. I think that's what my chil-dren will remember years from now too, decades after the toys and trinkets have disappeared in a dump somewhere. Father God wishes for the same thing. God chasers want God! Not even the "things of God" will satisfy someone who is a "man after God's own heart" (see Acts 13:22).

Most of the time when we get a visitation from God, our eyes are on the wrong thing. We want His spiritual "toys."[1] We tell Him, "Touch me, bless me, Father," and we have managed to turn our local churches into "bless me clubs." Nowhere in the Bible is the altar "the place of bless-ing." An altar exists for only one thing. Just ask that little lamb that was brought to the altar...this is not a place of blessing; it is a place of death. But if we can embrace *that* death, then perhaps we can see God's face.

Why Are You Talking About Death So Much?

I'm talking about the *New Testament equivalent of death,* which is repentance, brokenness, and humility before the Lord. Too many times we only give lip service to God's Word. We say it is true but we *act* like it isn't. What if God meant what He said? What if it's true that only dead men see His face?

We are too easily satisfied with things that are not quite what they ought to be. I'm pressing my point because the Church is in grave danger of once again stopping at the "burning bush" in this wonderful visitation of God's presence. There is a *greater* purpose behind the meetings taking place around the world (and it isn't just for us to get blessed). God wants to break open the heavens over our cities so the people who are without God will know that He is Lord and that He loves them. Now that is the true purpose of God's visitation among men. We need to get our eyes off the toys and onto the purpose....

Like Moses, we need to cry out, "No, thank You, Lord; that's not enough. We want more, we've got to see more, we want to see Your glory. *We don't want to see just where You have been; we want to see where You are going!*"

That is where we must stand, calling for God to show us where He's going to break open the heavens over our cities. That is what I'm looking for. I just want to find out where He's going so I can position myself at the place where He is going to break open. There is an element of sovereignty in God's choice of places. *Nobody on earth strikes the match for burning bushes.* Only God can do that. Our part consists of wandering through the wilderness until we find that spot, and then to remember to take off our shoes because we've stumbled onto holy ground.

I Can Almost Smell the Singed Fragrance...

Sometimes I visit places where I can almost smell the singed fragrance of leaves that don't burn. It makes me sense that we're near that place where God is going to give us an encapsulated vision of the greater purpose behind all this.

Most of what we have seen so far is the *renewal* of the Church. I'm thinking that *revival* is not the best word for what we are seeing because it refers to something that is dead being brought back to life. I don't have the terminology to describe what God is about to do. How do you describe a "tsunami"? How do you describe a tidal wave? How do you talk about what God can do, along with the unspeakable grace and strength that come with it?

The biblical model I desire and dream of is God's dealings with the city of Ninevah. I want to see a wave of God sweep through a city, pushing before it all of man's arrogance while leaving behind it nothing but a trail of broken repentance. I'm hungry for revival like we see in Jonah's description of citywide repentance and fasting in Ninevah.

That kind of revival *should have* happened at Nazareth but it didn't. Nazareth would have been the optimal place because that city had the greatest preacher who ever lived. Jesus stood in Nazareth's synagogue and said, "The Spirit of the Lord is upon Me." Then He read from the menu of what He wanted to do—heal the sick, open blind eyes, set the prisoners free—but He wasn't able to do any of it because of the unbelief of the people in Nazareth. We need to pay attention to this sad story because Nazareth was the "Bible belt" in Jesus' day. Nazareth was the place where it should have happened. (You cannot go by the outward appearance of a place or people.)

I don't care what a thing or a person looks like; only God knows His plans for the future. Many Christians have written off major metropolitan cities such as Los Angeles, New York, Detroit, Chicago, or Houston. Los Angeles may be the home of thousands of pornographic places and the Hollywood film industry, but Ninevah was an even more unlikely place for revival in its day! To say nothing of Shanghai, New Delhi, Calcutta, Rio de Janeiro...and the list grows! But if someone can find the light switch, His glory will flood these cities. It must, because He said that "the glory of God will cover the earth"! (See Numbers 14:21.)

I'm a Walking Dead Man

*O*nly dead men see God's face, so when you go behind that veil you have to say, "I'm really not alive anymore. I'm a walking dead man." When a condemned man begins his final walk to the death chamber, just before they close the door of the corridor, the warden or one of the chief guards will often shout through the hall, "*Dead man walking.*" This is to let everyone know that a man is spending his last few moments of life on this earth, and that they are to be still and honorable. The man is alive, but only for a few moments. When he gets to the death chamber, it's all over. That is how a Christian lives out Romans 12:1: *dead man walking.*

The high priest of old knew that he was a "dead man walking" when the other priests tied a rope around his ankle while he looked at the heavy veil separating him from the Holy of Holies. The only way he would ever walk out of that room alive was solely by the mercy and grace of God. We don't understand the delicate matter of approaching the glory of God today. We talk about the glory and say, "The glory is here," but it really isn't. The *anointing* is here, and there may be a measure of the light of God.

But if the glory of God ever showed up in full measure, we'd all be dead. Mountains melt at His manifest presence; how much more man's flesh![2]

We have failed to grasp something about the glory of God (perhaps we are unable to grasp it). Paul the apostle said, "That no flesh should glory in His presence" (1 Cor. 1:29). If there is flesh present when the glory of God comes, then it will have to be *dead* flesh, because nothing can live in that presence. The only mortal thing that can remain in His manifest presence and stand is "dead" flesh, because only dead men can see His face.

"I Don't Know If I'm Coming Back"

Once a year the high priest of Israel would leave his home with a heavy heart and tell his family, "I don't know if I'm coming back. I'm not sure, but I think I've done everything I'm supposed to do. Is my ephod on straight?" The Jews were so cautious about avoiding defilement that the high priest was not even allowed to sleep the night before he went behind the veil! The other priests kept him up all night reading the law to him, so that he wouldn't accidentally defile himself through a dream in the night.

Allegorically speaking, when the moment of truth finally came, the high priest would carefully dip his finger into the warm blood of the sacrificial goat or lamb and daub it on his earlobes. He would apply more blood to each of his thumbs and on his big toes. Why? Symbolically, he was taking on the appearance of one who is *dead* so he could come near God's glory and yet live. Once the blood of death was applied head and toe, the priest would take a deep breath and take one last look at the mortal realm, double-check the rope around his ankle, and reach for the censer. This bowl or container connected to a chain had hot embers in the bottom. The priest would take a handful of holy incense and drop it on top of the embers, which would create a thick billowing cloud of sweet-smelling smoke. The priest would stick this censer under the veil and swing it back and forth until smoke completely filled the Holy of Holies. Then he would gently lift the bottom hem of the heavy veil and crawl into the Most Holy Place with fear and trembling, desperately hoping he would come back alive. *Knees are better than feet for entering the Holy of Holies.*

The Aaronic Priests Knew Something We Do Not

The covering smoke was the priest's last-ditch fail-safe system to protect his living flesh from the consuming holiness of Almighty God. The Aaronic priests knew something about God that we need to redis-cover today. They knew that God is holy and mankind is not. They knew that living flesh would instantly die if it encountered the unshielded, uncovered glory of God. So when they went behind that veil, there had to be enough smoke in that room to hide everything from view—even though they had followed every requirement, covered themselves with blood, and stayed up all night reading the Scriptures. The way they knew the covering cloud was thick enough was if they couldn't see anything either. The priest had to fulfill all his duties, including the sprinkling of blood, by feel instead of by sight. The covering cloud was a reassuring sign to the man that he had a good chance of seeing the light of day again. (See Leviticus 16.)

I believe that the cloud of incense wasn't there just to keep the man from seeing God's glory. Perhaps it was be-cause if the Holy of Holies wasn't filled with smoke, then the glory of God would have an unimpeded view of "live flesh." There is a remarkable passage of Scripture that says, "And when he had opened the seventh seal, there was silence in heaven about the space of half an hour" (Rev. 8:1).

Why would the angels of Heaven stand in stunned silence for 30 minutes? The context of the previous chapter is the appearance of the saints arrayed in white robes standing before God Himself. There will come a day when our mortal bodies are going to take on immortality, when this corruption is going to take on incorruption. Yet even then, the residue of the flesh will still be there. I believe that when we step through the pearly gates, the angels are going to stand in stunned silence for 30 minutes, as if to say, "The redeemed are standing there, right in front of the Holy One." It's unimaginable to them that flesh can stand in the glory of God, but it can—if it's been transformed through the process of death and resurrection and through His shed blood. Only dead men can see God's face.

His Mercy Keeps Him Away From Us

*I*t is God's *mercy* that keeps Him away from us. For generation after generation, Christians have prayed strange little prayers and beat the altars saying, "God come near, God come near." I believe He has been answering us all along, but with a doubled-edged answer. With one hand, He beckons on, calling out to us, "Come on, call Me closer and I will come because I want to come near." Yet at the same time, He holds out His other hand in warning while saying, "Be careful, be careful. If you're going to get any closer, then make sure that everything is dead. If you really want to know Me, then everything must die."

Why did God audience death? What was it about the stench of the burning hair and hide of a sacrifice that was so inviting to God that it caused Him to literally leave Heaven and visit the place of a burning sacrifice? There is something about death that is inviting to God. You may not realize it, but death has been in every revival in Church history! Death was there in those early meetings on Azusa Street. Death was there in the First and Second Great Awakenings. The Pentecostal pioneer, Frank Bartleman, of the Azusa revival, said, "The depth of your repentance will determine the height of your revival."

The more death that God smells,
the closer He can come.

It's as if the smell of that sacrifice was a signal that God could draw near to His people for a moment without striking them down for their sin. His end goal has always been reunion and intimate communion with mankind, His highest creation; but sin made that a fatal affair. God cannot come close to living flesh because it reeks of the world. It has to be dead flesh for Him to come close. So when we beg for God to come close, He will, but He also says, "I can't really get any closer, because if I do, your flesh will be destroyed. I want you to understand that if you will just go ahead and die, then I can come near to you."

That is why repentance and brokenness—the New Testament equivalent of death—brings the manifest presence of God so near. But we want to avoid repentance because we don't like the smell of death. Anyone who has ever smelled the obnoxious odor of burning hair and hide will agree that it doesn't smell good. It isn't enticing to the senses of mankind, but it is very enticing to God because it is a signal that He can once again draw close to those He loves.

Forget the "High Entertainment Index"

The things that God likes and the things that we like are almost always two different things.

106

The Lord spoke to me one time while I was ministering and said, "Son, the services that I like, and the services that you like, are not the same." I began to notice that too often we categorically design our services to be man-pleasing services. We craft them to tickle the itching ear, and we want them to have a "high entertainment index." Unfortunately, these kinds of meetings have very little of our sacrificial love poured out to Him who alone deserves our praise and worship.

God would rather have moments with a few who really love Him than for everybody to come and be entertained. Yet we are hosting a party for God in which we trade presents with each other while totally ignoring *Him!* There is something about that element of *death to self* that is special. Maybe it's not very pleasing to us, and maybe we think it doesn't do anything for us or seem pleasing in our eyes, but it sure does something for God.

If you picked up this book hoping to get Holy Ghost chill-bumps up and down your spine, you may be disappointed. But if you opened these pages knowing in your heart that the Church needs a revolution in its worship and ways, then you won't be disappointed. The last time I read Psalm 103:1, it said, "Bless the Lord, O my soul." It did not say, "O my Lord, bless my soul." God is tired of just reaching into His pocket and dispensing the blessings of His hand. He wants us to enjoy the fellowship of His face, but only dead men can get close enough to see Him.

God Doesn't Dare Come Any Closer...

*M*ost of us are content to preserve some bit of our fallen life or fleshly ambitions while lightly clinging to the hem of God's garment of salvation. Oh, we can cling to the remnants of "our own thing" as long as we are willing to live on the handouts God is able to give us when He sticks His hand out from under the veil. It is only enough to keep us from spiritual famine, but God doesn't dare come any closer because it would kill the very flesh we prize so highly. The choice is ours.

God is looking for someone who is willing to tie a rope around an ankle and say, "If I perish, I perish; but I am going to see the king. I want to do everything I can to go behind that veil. I'm going to put on the blood, I'm going to repent, I'm going to do everything I can because I'm tired of knowing about Him. *I want to know Him. I've got to see His face.*"

No matter who you are, what you've done, or what religious tradition you embrace, the only way you are going to go through that veil is through the death of your flesh. The death of genuine repentance and brokenness before God will allow Him to draw near to you. The apostle Paul said, "For now we see through a glass, darkly; but then *face to face*: now I know in part; but then shall I know even as also I am known" (1 Cor. 13:12). At that point we will know God in the full measure of who He is, the way He knows us in the full measure of who we are.

The apostle John was exiled to the prison island of Patmos because of his faith in Christ, but I'm convinced there was a deeper reason for it. It was only after John was a walking dead man abandoned on a deserted island to die that he heard a voice and turned to look in the face of God the Son, Jesus Christ.

We all think we've known God and we all think we've been a part of the Church. But we need to look closely at John. This was the apostle who personally leaned on the breast of Jesus. He was the closest disciple. John watched Jesus awaken from a sound sleep to calm the storm on the Sea of Galilee. He saw Jesus literally stop a funeral procession to touch the body of a dead boy, raise him from the dead, and restore him to his mother. Yet this same apostle turned around on the island of Patmos and *saw Him* in His unveiled glory for the first time. He said that the Lord's head and hair were white like wool, and His eyes burned like fire. His feet were like fine brass. The Scriptures say that John fell at the Lord's feet *as though he were dead* (see Rev. 1:17). Why would John do that when he had already known Jesus for three years? In the visionary instant that John saw Him, he tasted death because he had seen life. It takes death to really see Him, and all I can say is, "It's a good day to die." The more I die, the closer He gets.

John the Baptist knew that secret too. Jesus said, "...Among them that are born of women there hath not risen a greater than John the Baptist" (Mt. 11:11a). Why? John had the grace to understand the little-known principle upon which all true ministry, service, and worship stand:

He must increase, but I must decrease (John 3:30).

If I decrease, then He can increase. Less of me means more of Him. John the Baptist was wise enough to acknowledge the true Giver of all gifts and abilities. He said, "A man can receive nothing, except it be given him from heaven" (Jn. 3:27b). Basically, if there is less of me, then there is room for more of Him. The more of me that dies, the closer He can get. How far can this go? Well, I don't know, but I can tell you the name of somebody to ask. Check with Enoch. He showed us that you can literally walk with God, but you will "die" along the way.

The Bible says, "And they overcame him by the blood of the Lamb, and by the word of their testimony; and they loved not their lives unto the death" (Rev. 12:11). Are you avoiding death? Do you want God's blessings on your life? The greatest blessing doesn't come from God's hand; it comes from His face in intimate relationship. When you finally see Him and know Him, you have come to the source of all power.

It's Not Going to Be a Cheap Blessing

It is true that all flesh must die in the presence of His glory, but it is also true that all that is of the Spirit *lives forever* in His glory. The eternal part of your being that really wants to live can live forever, but first there is something about your flesh that has to die. Your flesh holds you back from the glory of God, so you are most likely locked in an unending wrestling match between the flesh and the spirit as you read these words. It is time for you to just go ahead and tell Him, "Lord, I want to see Your glory." The God of Moses is willing to reveal Himself to you but it's not going to be a cheap blessing. You will have to lie down and die. He can only come close to you to the degree you are willing to die.

You need to forget who's around you and abandon the "normal protocol." God is in the business of re-defining what we call "church" anyway. He's looking for people who are hot after His heart. He wants a Church of Davids who are *after* His own heart[3] (not just His hand). You can seek for His blessing and play with His toys, or you can say, "No, Daddy, I don't just want the blessings; I want You. I want You to come close. I want You to touch my eyes, touch my heart, touch my ears, and change me, Lord. I'm tired of me the way I am, because if I can change, *then the cities can change too.*"

We need to pray for a breakthrough, but we cannot pray for a breakthrough unless we're broken ourselves. Breakthroughs only come to broken people who are not pursuing their own ambition, but who are after the purposes of God. We need to weep over our city just as Jesus wept over Jerusalem. We need a breakthrough from the Lord.

Don't resist the Holy Spirit when the hand of God tries to mold your heart. The Potter of your soul is simply trying to "soften" you. He wants to bring you to such a place of tenderness that it doesn't take a hurricane-force wind from Heaven for you to even know that He is present. He wants you to be so tender that the gentlest breeze from Heaven, the smallest zephyr from His presence, will set your heart a-dancing, and you'll say, "It's Him!"

We Want Life, But God Is Looking for Death

*W*e need to repent for designing services that men like, instead of yielding to what God likes. Like most men and women, we have wanted "life" in our services when God was after "death" in our gatherings! It is "death" through repentance and brokenness that ushers in the presence of God and causes you to draw near to the Lord and yet *live*.

Some people get very uncomfortable at this point because it's starting to smell a little smoky. They can smell the odor of burning flesh in the air. It may not smell good to us, but God is drawn toward repentance. The Bible says, "When a sinner repents, the angels rejoice" (see Lk. 15:10). Death and repentance on earth bring about joy in the heavenlies.

Revival must begin in your local church before it can reach into your community. If you are hungry for revival, then I have a word from the Lord for you: *Fire doesn't fall on empty altars.* There has to be a sacrifice on the altar for the fire to fall. If you want the fire of God, you must become the fuel of God. Jesus sacrificed Himself to win our salvation, but He has called each and every person who wants to follow Him to do what? To lay down their lives and *take up their cross* and follow Him.[4] According to

Strong's Concordance, the Greek word for "cross," *stauros*, means "figuratively, exposure to death, i.e. self-denial."[5] Elijah didn't ask for God's fire to fall down on the altar until he had loaded it up with fuel and a worthy sacrifice. We've been praying for the fire to fall, but there's nothing on the altar!

If you are hungry for the fire to fall in your church, then you need to just crawl up on the altar and say, "God, whatever it takes. I lay myself on the altar and ask You to consume me with Your fire, Lord." Then we can follow the lead of John Wesley who explained how he drew such large crowds during the First Great Awakening:

"I set myself on fire, and the people come to see me burn."

≋ Notes from those on the chase ≋

*A few weeks ago, I came home from church and cried all day. There was this feeling inside that there had to be more. Even though I am a young minister (I've been licensed for a year) who loves God, I got overwhelmed this particular day with a sense of needing to really know God...About two weeks after that session, I went to a friend's house. She had **The God Chasers** on her bookshelf. As I read the back and looked at some of the chapter titles, I thought to myself, I don't believe this. She let me borrow the book. I have been in tears as I have been reading. I don't believe that someone has written a book about what I was feeling.*

I want to be a God Chaser. I don't just want His hand, His toys. I really want God's heart. I expect to see His face (or at least be in His glory).

—Angela B.

≋   ≋

*Your book was given to my husband by a young college lady who was stranded on the side of the road when her car died on her. My husband offered to take her back to college, 25 miles away, as she had no money to get other transportation and no one she could call. The young lady told my husband that although she could not repay him, she wanted him to have a book that she had carried with her. The book was **The God Chasers**. He gladly brought the book home, and I saw it on the counter. I picked it up immediately and began reading. As soon as I began reading the book, I could not stop to put it down. You see, I have been a Christian for more than five years now, and although at one time three years ago I had experienced just a touch of the glory of God, I had not done so since. Your book opened my eyes to many areas of my Christian walk that I*

*had been missing. I had tried to read the Bible from begin-
ning to end thinking that that maybe would help give me the
boost I needed. When that did not work, I began feeling that
maybe I was even in the wrong church. I just wanted to be
in the place that I had once experienced, a place that words
can never describe. From the moment I began reading your
book, I could not put it down. Everything in your book lined
up with where I was missing it. As I began to press in and
meditate on those principles that are in your book, an im-
mediate change took place. While following your principle
of intercession, within two weeks a change had occurred in
our church like never before. Now people all over are falling
to their faces in true repentance, and the desire to just meet
the Master and get one touch of His glory is throughout our
local church. My desire to know God and have the passionate relationship continues to grow stronger and stronger
each day. I cannot describe the things that have happened
to me and what I have seen in others. It is truly "strange"
from the physical sense, but when I get in even just a small
presence of God, I could care less what others think. The
experience in His presence is so real and awesome that it
outweighs any other thing imaginable. Although I had de-
sired to be at that place I was once before, the Lord has
shown me that it was the past and that I have not even experienced the place that He desires for me to be. I have
passed that place where I once was and have experienced a
deeper place, many miles from where I thought was "the"
place to be. And my desire to be even closer continues like
fuel on a flame.*

—no name

Ask Some Questions

1. Can you think of a Bible character who needed a break-through? Where in your life do you need a breakthrough? *Often it is that very place where you need to be broken.* Brokenness to breakthrough can be a daily experience. What patterns in your life need to be broken? Repent! Die to your self and allow God to rebuild that area of your life.

2. God's logic is very different from man's logic.
   I must decrease so that God can increase (see Jn. 3:30).
   If you want to keep your life, you must lose it (see Mt. 16:25).
   If you want to be great, become servant to all (see Mk. 10:43-45).
   Have you ever faced a time of decrease in your life? How did it feel? Did you experience God's power and presence increasing in the midst of or following that time?

3. Think of a Bible character who wanted to please himself and not God. Now think about areas in your own life where you are trying to win the favor of people. In what areas are you trying to please yourself?

Endnotes

1. I'm using the term *toys* to describe our attitude toward God's gifts. I am not trying to demean or belittle the genuine purpose and value of these supernatural impartations from God. God did not give us precious gifts such as the gift of prophecy, the gift of the word of knowledge, or the gift of healings to use to impress flesh or influence people. They are given for the purpose of edifying and equipping the Body of Christ for the work of the ministry.

2. See Judg. 5:5; Nahum 1:5.

3. See Acts 13:22.

4. See Lk. 9:23.

5. James Strong, *Strong's Exhaustive Concordance of the Bible* (Peabody, MA: Hendrickson Publishers, n.d.), **cross** (#G4716).

Chapter 5

Do We Run Away
Or Go In?

A chance to meet the One you always knew was there

Whenever I encounter a party scene or see people drinking and acting like pure pagans, *I can't help but like them!* They don't play any religious games. They know who and what they are. (The ones who irritate me are the ones who play games and pretend to be something they are not!) Almost every time I pass by a bar or nightclub, the crazy thought comes to mind, *Lord, why not right here? Why don't You just break out right here?*

My definition of revival is when God's glory breaks out of the four walls of our churches to flow through the streets of the city. Revival of historical proportions in modern times would be when God invades the shopping malls on Friday night. I want to see every mall association be forced to hire full-time chaplains just to handle the crowds of people they find weeping under conviction each shopping day. I want to see citywide calls for volunteer ministers just to handle the flood of people who get convicted of their sins when they pass through the town. (Security guards know what to do with shoplifters, but would they know what to do with people who come up to them in distress because they've been convicted of their sin?) Hasten the day!

I believe God has stirred such a pent-up demand for His presence that in the "day of the Lord" (if His people will pursue His presence), the existing churches will not be able to handle the explosion of lost souls wanting to be saved. The modern Church is a caretaker or a maintenance organization at best, and a museum of what once was, at worst. Our greatest problem is that we've "stocked our shelves" with the wrong stuff. We offer the hungry our dusty shelves of bland, man-produced religious ritual that no one in his right mind is really hungry for! Empty religious ritual is as appetizing as "blue mashed potatoes" or some other unnatural concoction. If anybody could ever open a store that just dispenses Jesus, the hungry masses would come. Perhaps the reason we haven't stocked our services with the right stuff is because it doesn't come cheap.

The Church today has made it to the halfway point in its journey across the wilderness. We are camped at the foot of Mount Sinai, much like the children of Israel in the Book of Exodus. It is obvious that we have reached the point where we are going to have to make a decision. Will we go in or run away?

And Moses went up unto God, and the Lord called unto him out of the mountain, saying, Thus shalt thou say to the house of Jacob, and tell the children of Israel;

118

Ye have seen what I did unto the Egyptians, and how I bare you on eagles' wings, and brought you unto Myself.

Now therefore, if ye will obey My voice indeed, and keep My covenant, then ye shall be a peculiar treasure unto Me above all people: for all the earth is Mine:

And ye shall be unto Me a kingdom of priests, and an holy nation. These are the words which thou shalt speak unto the children of Israel (Exodus 19:3-6).

This is New Testament language on the pages of the Old Testament. They were given the obvious option of leap-frogging to a new level of intimacy.[1]

We've Come to a Mountain of Decision

We can be contented with burning bushes and rejoice over our first encounters with the supernatural God. We can be satisfied with the God-carved tablets of revelation and wisdom and all the other things that He does. But now we've come to a mountain of decision, the proverbial "fork in the road." God has pulled us out of sin and out of the world. He has begun to make a people out of us. That's what the journey in the wilderness was all about; God was making a people out of "no people."

Peter wrote, "Which in time past were *not a people*, but are now *the people of God*: which had not obtained mercy, but now have obtained mercy" (1 Pet. 2:10). God took slaves and menial servants who had no education and certainly no self-esteem, and He planted His own character in them and placed His name on them. He pulled them out of Egypt and said, "Now, I'm going to make a *people* out of you." He was literally building a Bride.

The Lord brought the descendants of Abraham to the base of Mount Sinai, but it wasn't easy. When the multitude

119

of people needed food, God wanted them to seek Him for their bread, but instead they berated Moses and talked about how good it was back in Egypt, the place of their bondage. Nevertheless, Moses prayed and God supplied quail and manna. The same thing happened when there was a water shortage. Instead of asking God or believing in His abundant supply, they immediately cornered Moses to complain and talk about the "good old days" in Egypt. God had something better for the children of Israel, but it was almost as if He was thinking, *If I can just get them past this mountain, then I can have hope of taking them all the way.*

Called to "A Place in Him"

The sad and unfortunate truth of the Book of Exodus is that the motley group of people God brought to Mount Sinai was *not the group of people* that He took across the river Jordan into the promised land. *Something happened at the mountain.* God called them and made them a nation for the first time in their history. He called them to a place—a place of blessing and a place of change—where they didn't want to go. Don't fall into the trap of thinking that this "place" was merely some physical spot on the map, because these people were already traipsing across the wilderness. Their blessing didn't consist of some rocky real estate someplace, although the promised land was part of the package deal. God called them to *a promised place in Him.* He called them to a place of covenant, a place of intimacy with their Creator that was not offered to any other people on the planet at that time. *That's the secret of the secret place.* We think that the idea of a "kingdom of priests" is an exclusively New Testament or Christian idea, but it was also God's original plan for Israel!

120

And the Lord said unto Moses, Go unto the people, and sanctify them to day and to morrow, and let them wash their clothes,

*And be ready against the third day: **for the third day the Lord will come down in the sight of all the people** upon mount Sinai.*

*...when the trumpet soundeth long, **they shall come up to the mount*** (Exodus 19:10-11,13b).

Although the first generation of Israelites gathered around the mountain would ultimately believe the fearful spies and shrink away from the promised land in fear, the real cause of their failure is found right there at the foot of Mount Sinai. God intended for *all* the Israelites to come *close to Him* on the mountain, but they were uncomfortable.

*And all the people saw the thunderings, and the lightnings, and the noise of the trumpet, and the mountain smoking: and when the people saw it, **they removed, and stood afar off.***

*And they said unto Moses, Speak thou with us, and we will hear: but **let not God speak with us, lest we die.***

And Moses said unto the people, Fear not: for God is come to prove you, and that His fear may be before your faces, that ye sin not.

*And **the people stood afar off**, and **Moses drew near** unto the thick darkness where God was* (Exodus 20:18-21).

They saw the lightning and heard the thunder, and they shrank back in fear. They ran from His presence instead of pursuing Him as Moses did. They were unhappy with the style of leadership that God had chosen. (He couldn't lay down His identity as the Almighty God just to please man then, and He won't do it today either.) So the end result of their flight from holy intimacy that day was that they died before they or their children ever entered the promised land. *They preferred distant respect over intimate relationship.*

It wasn't God's original plan for the first generation of Israelites to die in the wilderness. He wanted to take the same group of people whom He brought out of the land of bondage into the land of promise. He wanted to give His new nation of former slaves their very own land and inheritance, but they wouldn't have it because of fear and unbelief. Their doom was sealed when they looked across the Jordan at the promised land and shrank back, but it really began when they shrank back from God's presence in the cloud on Mount Sinai. It was there that they ran from God and demanded that Moses stand between them. (The Church has been suffering from the same problem ever since.) We often prefer that a man stand between us and God. We have a hell-inspired, fleshly fear of holy intimacy with God. The roots of this fear reach all the way back to the Garden of Eden. Adam and Eve hid in shameful fear while God longed for sweet fellowship.

Do We Run Away Or Go On In?

Now look closely at your local church. I can almost guarantee you that some of the people in the congregation were there "in the beginning." Others came a few months later or several years later. Some are brand-new believers or at least new arrivals. God has brought all of you to the mountain today. You who were "not a people," have been made a people. God took all of us out of the slavery of sin. He's pulled some of us out of bad marriages. Others were delivered from the bondage of alcoholism and other chronic substance-abuse problems. We've been delivered from joblessness and destitution, chronic depression, and too many other pits of hell to mention. In the end, we have all wound up together at the foot of His mountain hearing His call to come closer. Now we face the same challenge as the children of Israel thousands of years ago: Do we run away or go in? Into what? Into His presence.

There is an air of expectancy and excitement in the Church today. You probably sense that "it's not too much further" as I do. Some scholars believe that when the Israelites stood at the foot of Mount Sinai, they were only a few days' march away from the promised land. The only reason they were delayed was because of their reluctance to press in to God. Their fear of intimacy sowed the seeds for fear of the enemy. The same can be said of most churches today. I really sense that we stand at a critical crossroads today.

On the one hand, we could say, "We've come too far to turn around now." But we could also say, "We're really tired. We want to sit here for a while." The real question is, What does God say? I believe He wants us to grasp where we are at this point. He wants us to reach out and receive everything He has to give us for today.

You and I are going to do one of two things from this point on:

1. We will grow into a relationship with Him, no matter what it costs us, or,

2. We will turn back to where we came from and become a program-driven, meeting-going, organizing, committee-run church people, doing all the "good" things that "good people" are supposed to do. We will end up fondly looking back on this time of decision and saying, "Those were the days."

I don't know about you, but I don't want to grow old and look back with regret someday and say, "Oh, those were great days." Why should I when I've come to understand that with God I can live in the present tense? I can walk in the freshness of what He has for me *every* day. If we dare to follow God today, then on some tomorrow we may be able to look back and say, "I remember those years; that was *before* we had the great revival of His presence!"

Our Future Depends on Our Outlook

Frankly, our future depends on our outlook in this hour of decision. If our outlook is, "Well, we've done pretty well," then this is probably all we'll do. But our futures will look totally different if we say, "Thank You, Lord...but *where's the rest*? There's got to be more! Show me Your glory!"

Satan's most successful trick is to get us to race to false finish lines. He works tirelessly to get us to stop short and say, "We made it!" He delights when he sees us fall or pull over to the wayside only to notice at the last moment that *the finish line is still ahead*. The apostle knew of what he spoke when he said, "I press toward the mark, forgetting those things that are behind" (see Phil. 3:13-14).

We need to learn from the events at Mount Sinai. It was there that the Israelites built the tabernacle according to the instructions God gave to Moses. It was on Mount Sinai that God gave to Moses the great revelation of His law in the Ten Commandments. But other equally important things happened there as well. It was also there that a golden calf of idolatry was created.

First of all, God revealed on Mount Sinai that He wanted to begin dealing with the people *directly* and personally. Until that day, Moses had always relayed to the Israelites everything that God said. That was a time of transition, a period in which God was saying, "Okay, it's time to grow up. I want to talk to you directly from now on as an entire nation of holy priests. I don't want to have any more intermediaries. I love Moses, but I don't want to have to speak through him to reach you. I want to deal with you directly as My nation, as My people."

Many Have Become "Milk Babies" in Padded Pews

*U*nfortunately, the Israelites suffered from the same problem many Christians do today. We have become addicted to the anointing, the relayed word of good preaching and teaching. Too many of us have become "milk babies" who want to sit on padded pews in an air-conditioned and climate-controlled building where someone else will pre-digest what God has to say and then regurgitate it back to us in a half-digested form. (We're afraid of getting "spiritual indigestion" from messages we think are "too rough" to handle.) *Tender tummies are unused to tough truth!*

The solution is hunger and desperation for God Himself without intermediaries. We need to pray, "God, I'm tired of everybody else hearing from You! Where is the lock on my prayer closet? I'm going to lock myself away until I hear from You for myself!"

We make a great deal out of reading the Word and that is important. But we need to remember that the early Church didn't have access to what we call the New Testament for many years. They didn't even have the Old Testament Scriptures because those expensive scrolls were locked up in synagogues. The only Scriptures they had were the verses from the law, the Psalms, and the prophets that had been passed down orally from grandfathers and grandmothers—and that only if they were Jewish believers.

125

So what *did* they have? They walked and talked with *Him* in such a rich level of intimacy that it wasn't necessary for them to pour over dusty love letters that were written long ago. They had God's love notes freshly written on their hearts.[2]

The Holy Spirit is saying, "Look, I know it's great that I've brought you out of sin and your clothes aren't wearing out. You are living in a measure of blessing, and you have My presence revealed in the cloud and the fire every day. I know you've got good leadership, but what *I* really want is this: I want to grow you up and I want to pull you close in a new level of intimacy."

No true revival has ever occurred simply because people sought revival. They were birthed when people *sought Him*. In our presumptuous thinking, we have said, "Okay, we're going to hold a revival." You might as well try to hold a hurricane! If you can hold it, then "it ain't revival." If you can contain it or control it, then "it ain't revival either." We need to call it what it is: a series of good meetings complete with whipped-cream preaching and maraschino cherries of man on top! We may love it and lick our lips through every minute of it, *but it isn't revival.* We have to face the fact that we have become addicted to all the things that accompany church, like the choirs and the music. But they are not what God calls "church" and they are not true revival either. I have a strong sense that God is about to strip all that away to ask us, "Now, who loves *Me*? Who wants *Me*?" It's time to seek the Reviver instead of revival!

God is tired of having *long distance relationships* with His people. He was tired of it thousands of years ago in Moses' day, and He is tired of it today. He really wants to have intimate, close encounters with you and me. He wants to invade our homes with His abiding presence in a way that will make every visitor begin to weep with wonder and worship the moment they enter.

Run Away Or Go In

*And all the people saw the thunderings, and the lightnings, and the noise of the trumpet, and the mountain smoking: and when the people saw it, **they removed, and stood afar off.***
*And **the people stood afar off**, and **Moses drew near** unto the thick darkness where God was* (Exodus 20:18, 21).

What a divine dichotomy! One ran in; the other ran away!

God was calling the people to intimacy and they ran the other way! They told Moses, "...let not God speak with us, *lest we die*" (Ex. 20:19). They understood that only things that match the character of God as depicted in the Ten Commandments could stand to live in His presence. By running away, they were saying, "Look, we don't want to live up to that. Don't let God talk to us right now." All God wanted them to do when He gave Moses the Ten Commandments was to clean up their act so He could do more than just see them from a distance. He wanted to walk with them once again in the cool of the desert day. He wanted to sit with them and share His heart in intimate communion. Nothing has changed, my friend. He wants to do the same thing now with you and me. Our proper response is, "Please, God, speak with us *even if we have to die!*"

The sad reality may be that most Christians in America don't have a real sense of the abiding presence of God because they refuse to clean up the clutter in their lives. And many of us who attempt to clear the clutter tend to get stuck in the logjam of legalism.

Hearing Father's Footsteps

*W*hen the Israelites told Moses that they were afraid, he tried to explain to them, "Fear not, God is only trying to prove you. That thunder and lightning reminds you of His awesome power so that you won't sin. You see, He's just wanting you to come clean so He can talk with you" (see Ex. 20:20). Isn't it amazing how ponderous and heavy your parents' footsteps seemed to be when you heard them come in your direction, especially at those times when you were doing something you shouldn't have been doing? The Israelites were hearing Father's footsteps.

The Bible says, "And the people stood afar off," while "Moses drew near unto the thick darkness where God was" (Ex. 20:21). What a picture. The people are running this way while Moses is running that way, saying, "Come on, guys, it's God. He's just saying, 'Come near to Me.' He's never done this before. When I was up on the mountain He let me get this close, and now He's come down because He wants all of us to draw near to Him together."

God always starts with the leadership, and Moses had already stepped into that thick darkness once before on the mountaintop. At this point, God wanted the rest of the Israelites to join Moses in His presence, but they ran away instead. It appears to me that the history of the Jewish people went downhill from the moment God said, "Come near," and they said, "No way." And it is abundantly clear that this problem isn't unique to the Israelites of Moses' day—it is also a serious problem in the Church today.

All They Want to Do Is "Date" God

*T*here is something in us that makes us afraid of the commitment that comes with real intimacy with God. For one thing, intimacy with God requires *purity*. The days of fun and games in the Church are over. What do I mean by "fun and games"? If your definition of fun is "low commitment and lots of thrills and chills," then all you've ever wanted to do is "date God." You just wanted to get in the backseat with Him. Do I need to draw a picture? God is tired of us wanting to get our thrills from Him without putting on the ring of commitment! Some are more enamored with the "goose bumps" than the glory! They're addicted to the anointing, liking the feeling of being blessed, receiving the "gifts" like a religious "gold-digger," happy with chocolates, flowers, and jewelry. The last time I checked, He was still looking for a bride, not a girlfriend; one who will "stick" with Him.

I'm afraid that many people in the Church have simply approached God to get what they can from Him without committing anything in return. God is saying to His Church, "I don't want that. Now if you want to marry Me, let's do this right. Let's pledge ourselves to each other." We've chased after cheap thrills without the commitment, but God is saying, "Intimacy." And He's saying it everywhere: "Intimacy." And *out of that intimacy* will come revival. The babe of revival is hewn from the granite rock of commitment to the Bridegroom. Babies are always birthed from intimacy. It's time to "draw near."

We've often placed the cart before the horse. We say, "We want revival," and never mention intimacy. We seek revival without seeking *Him*. That's a lot like some stranger of the opposite sex walking up to you and saying, "I want kids. What do you say? I don't really know you and

I'm not even sure I like you. Of course, I don't want all the commitment that goes with marriage, but I really do want children. How about it?"

Leaders in the Church have written countless books on how to grow churches, but sometimes the underlying message there is, "This is how to grow churches without relationship with Him." We have tried to find shortcuts to short-circuit the "intimacy requirement" every way we can. Why? It is because what we want is a "bunch of kids" sitting on the pews in the church so we can look around and compare with everybody else's church family in town. Children in and of themselves do not make a household! They are the natural by-product of a loving relationship and intimacy in a marriage. Frankly, most of our churches today are the spiritual equivalent of a dysfunctional household—"single parent" presbyteries. Where is "Dad"?

What we really need to be seeking is a *real relationship with God*. Anytime you put a man and a woman together who love each other, you don't have to worry about whether or not they will have children in most cases. It's a natural outgrowth of the process of intimacy.

Why is it that the largest revivals in the last century have never been held on American soil? I think it dates to the era when our morals went down the tubes along with our commitment levels. I propose that our nation's collective ability to really grow deep in its relationship with God is accurately mirrored in its reciprocal (or opposite) factor—by our skyrocketing trend toward rampant divorce rates and broken marriages. In other words, we have forgotten or dismissed as unimportant the lost art of commitment to God. As we made the choice to turn away from God's face at the mountain, every other commitment in our lives began to deteriorate and fall apart as well.

Hothouse Christians Have No Root

*M*ost Christians in North America are "hot-house Christians" who bloom as long as they are kept in a protected and carefully controlled environment far from fear, distress, or persecution. "God forbid that it should 'cost' us something to speak the name of Jesus."

But time and again, we have seen that if you take hothouse Christians out of their protected environment and put them into the real world where the wind of adversity blows and the rain of sorrow falls; if they have to endure the hot sun and the drought it brings, then they discover that they never developed a root system in the hothouse. So they wither and say, "I'm just not cut out for this!"

God has dealt with me to the point where I have been forced to redefine some of my criteria for what it means to be "saved." If it takes the "perfection of environment" to prove the presence of God in your life, then my guess is that the persecuted Christians just don't have God. How can they? They don't have Bible seminars; they don't have choirs or the latest worship music. They don't have air conditioning, ushers, nurseries, electronic paging systems, carpeted sanctuaries, or staff counselors. Their worship environment is terrible. If they get caught having church, they must pay a terrible price. I read an account of a group of Chinese Christians who were caught holding a church service. The officials placed a horse trough in the middle of town and forced every man and woman in that congregation to urinate into it. Then they drowned the pastor in it, right in front of their eyes!

Do you know what happened? The church congregation doubled in two weeks, and it wasn't because of their nice sanctuary or dynamic worship team. True church growth, wherever it may be, in freedom or persecution, comes because of only one thing. It springs forth from an intimate knowledge of the living God.

The Confession of People in Love

These kinds of believers don't gauge their relationship with God by whether they received a salary raise this quarter, by how things are going with their bank account, or by how much "fun" they've had during church activities. They have joined Paul by saying, "But none of these things move me, *neither count I my life dear unto myself*, so that I might finish my course with joy, and the ministry, which I have received of the Lord Jesus, to testify the gospel of the grace of God" (Acts 20:24). This is the confession of people in love and in intimate communion with their Maker.

God is calling. The first time God revealed this to me, I trembled and wept in front of the people as I told them the same thing I tell you today: "You are at Mount Sinai today, and God is calling you into personal intimacy with Him. If you dare to answer His call, then it is going to redefine everything you've ever done." Your decision today will determine whether you go forward or backward in your walk with Christ.

Intimacy with God requires a certain level of brokenness because purity comes from brokenness. The games are over, friend. He's calling you.

Could it be that we don't want to get into that cloud with God because we know He's going to look into our hearts, and we know what He will find there? We have to deal with more than our outward actions; we have to deal with our inward motives also. We must come clean, because God can't reveal His face to a partially pure Church. It would be destroyed in an instant.

132

God is calling people who want serious revival into a place of transparent purity. It's *you* who He's after. He wants you to draw near, but at the same time, if you come near, then He will have to deal with you. That can only mean one thing: You must die. This is the same God who told Moses, "No man has seen My face and lived." So remember to pass by the altar of forgiveness and sacrifice on your way into the Holy of Holies. It's time for us to lay our egos on the cross, to crucify our will, to lay our own agendas aside.

God is calling you to a higher level of commitment. Forget the plans you've made for yourself and lay on His altar and die to self. Pray, "God, what do You want me to do?" It's time to lay everything aside and cover yourself in the blood. Nothing alive can stand in His presence. But if you're dead, then He will make you alive. So all you need to do is die if you really want to get into His presence. When the apostle Paul wrote, "I die daily," he was saying, "I enter into the presence of God every day" (see 1 Cor. 15:31b). Run in, don't run away!

⚈ Notes from those on the chase ⚈

*F*irst let me say that I am a Roman Catholic. I read **The God Chasers**, and I am recommending it to all my Catholic friends. God has done a great work through you if you've written a book that I would even endorse. I'm an ecumenistic person, and I believe that there a lot of Protestant folks out there who on the outside say, "Hi, how are you doing?" with a big smile and are all cordial, but who don't believe that there are any Spirit-filled Catholics out here, that the Pope is the antichrist, and that we are all going to hell. (Of course, there also are those who will lock arms and go to the depths of hell with us, to kick satan's behind, too!) So when I read a book by a Protestant author, I look for overt proselytizational statements, and then I read through it for the covert ones.

The blessing is that you were about God Chasing, and that was it. It didn't make any difference what church you belong to; it was about repentance and seeking the face of God. I was very blessed, and I am an intensified God Chaser now!

—Donald L.

⚈   ⚈

I felt compelled to write you after reading your book, **The God Chasers**. It lit a fire in me that was only a small flame before. More people need to think and spread God's Word the way you do. I can only imagine the lives you've changed through your words...I am a 22-year-old single girl, living by myself. More importantly, I am a new Christian...It's always been important to me to go to a church that is led by the Holy Ghost, not a program. I have such a hunger for God's Word...After reading your book, my hunger has reached an uncontrollable state. I want to spread your message...

—Tiffany A.

Ask Some Questions

1. How did God make "a people" out of the Israelites? How is God calling us to become "a people"? Do your family members and coworkers see you as one of God's people?

2. How do you gauge how close you are to God? Is it by the blessings you receive? By what standards should you gauge your relationship to Him?

3. Why did the Israelites run from an encounter with God? Why do we run away from God? Why are we afraid to deal directly with God?

Endnotes

1. See 1 Pet. 2:9.

2. Let me hasten to add that my statements here are not meant to imply that I feel the Bible is unnecessary or irrelevant, or anything less than the anointed, inerrant, and infallible Word of God. My purpose here is to caution Christians against the practice of reading the Bible in a permanent state of "past tense" perspective. "Look what God did *back then with those people.* Too bad He doesn't do that today with us." God's Word is a road map to something greater—*the God of the Word.* Sometimes I think we almost fall into idolatry when we tend to worship the Word of our God more than the God of the Word.

Chapter 6

How to Handle the Holy

Moving from anointing to glory

"Do you quietly bow your head in reverence
when you step into the average church?
I would be surprised if your answer is yes."
A.W. Tozer

My life changed forever on the October weekend in Houston, Texas, when God's presence invaded the atmosphere like a thunderbolt and split the podium at the Sunday service. I'll never forget telling my friend, the pastor, "You know, *God could have killed you.*" I wasn't laughing when I said it. It was as if God had said, "I'm here and I want you to *respect* My presence." A picture of Uzzah's grave had popped into my mind.

We didn't know what we were asking for when we said we "wanted God." I know I thought I did, but I didn't. When God actually showed up, none of us were prepared for the reality of His presence. As I've already mentioned earlier in this book, there was very little preaching because we didn't have a choice. God repossessed His church for a period of time and He wouldn't allow anything to happen that He hadn't specifically ordained for that service.

The thick blanket of His tangible presence was so heavy that I received an "up close and personal" understanding of what is meant by God's Word when it says:

> *And it came to pass, when the priests were come out of the holy place, that the cloud filled the house of the Lord,*
> *So that the priests could not stand to minister because of the cloud: for the glory of the Lord had filled the house of the Lord* (1 Kings 8:10-11).

God came so suddenly and so forcefully into that church building that we were afraid to do anything unless He specifically told us to do it. His presence was always there of course, but not the weighty manifest presence we experienced at certain times. In those moments, all we could do was sit there, trembling. We were afraid to take an offering without specific permission from God. We kept asking each other, "Do you think it's okay to take an offering? Do you think we should do this? What about that?"

Reverence the Holy

*W*hy were we so hesitant about things most of us had done thousands of times before? We were *amateurs at handling the holy.* (We still are!) I have noticed that early on in visitations of God's manifest presence, He comes suddenly and without warning. But in subsequent visitations, He comes only by invitation (displayed hunger). The crux of the whole matter is simple: Do you really want Him to come? Are you willing to pay the cost of becoming a God chaser? Then you will have to learn how to properly reverence, handle, and steward the holiness of God.

A.W. Tozer was deeply concerned about our loss of holiness in the Church. He noticed that the average church was losing that sense of sacredness in their worship services, and it grieved him. To him, that lack of reverence meant that people didn't think God's presence was in their church. (And it probably wasn't.) Tozer observed that the yearning and desiring of a spiritual life was losing out to worldly secularism. Such an environment does not produce revival. As a result, Tozer felt that God may actually look elsewhere if the Church does not come back to Him, to a relationship with *Him*, and not just His "stuff."[1]

I now know why the high priests of old would say to their fellow priests, "Tie a rope around my ankle, because I'm going into the place where the glory of God abides. I've done everything I know to make myself ready, but I am in awe of God." I'm not afraid of God; I love Him. But I now have a respect for the glory and the holy things of God that I confess I didn't have before.

It used to be easy to handle the anointing, but now I know it is a sacred thing. Now I am careful to pray two things before I minister in most cases: I pray a prayer of thanksgiving first of all, saying, "Thank You, Lord, for visiting us." Then I ask the second part of that prayer, "Please stay, Lord."

If you remember the barren woman who prepared the prophet's room for Elijah in Second Kings chapter 4, she was rewarded with a son. When satan took him away in premature death, God sent the prophet to raise him back to life. Satan cannot steal what God has birthed, but God will only birth things *to people who make room for the miraculous* by faith. That is why I am careful to thank the

Lord for coming, and then I tell Him that *we have made provisions for Him* to come again. "Lord, we're going to be here worshiping You on Wednesday, Thursday, and Friday. Our sole purpose is to praise Your name and seek Your lovely face." By faith I believe that God will visit us once again. I know from His Word that when God visits someone, He causes new and precious things to be born. And even if satan tries to kill them, God will move Heaven and earth to breathe life back into what He has birthed!

We need to learn how to handle the holy things of God with greater tenderness and sensitivity. We must remember that "the good" can quickly become the worst enemy of "the best." If you want God's best, then you will have to sacrifice what you think is good and acceptable. If you and I can find out what is acceptable to *Him*, "the best," then the promise of visitation becomes real.

I think I've seen a glimpse of what I think God is doing. *He is moving into position.*

Going to Where God's Glory Belongs

*C*hapter 13 of the Book of First Chronicles tells us that after David was crowned king over Israel and defeated the Philistines, he decided to move the ark of the covenant back to Jerusalem. This was a "move of God" in the sense that this Old Testament abode of the manifest presence of God was being moved from its interim resting place to *the place where His glory belonged.* God is wanting to move into His true resting place. Jerusalem is spoken of as a type and shadow of the Church. The apostle Paul spoke of Jerusalem "which is above" as the "mother of us all," referring allegorically to the Church (see Gal. 4:26). This is a picture of the Church, the spiritual city or abode of God. God wants His glory in the Church, on display for the world to see.

There were times when God's glory, His *kabod* (or "weighty presence") was moved out of its rightful place through the sin or indifference of men. The grandson of the old priest, Eli, remains an eternal landmark of God's absence from man's worst-laid plans. As the newborn boy's mother lay dying, she told the women at her side that the boy would be named *Ichabod*, which literally means "the glory has departed." Her labor began moments after she learned that the ark of God had been taken by the Philistines in battle and that her husband, Phinehas, was slain. Eli's sons, Phinehas and Hophni, had sinned against God even while attending to their priestly duties before the Lord! (Is this *still* the case today in countless ministries? The same fate may well await them—their legacy may well be remembered under the name "Ichabod, the glory has departed.")

In the 20 years or so that passed after the loss of the ark, Saul the king never showed any interest in bringing the ark of the covenant to Jerusalem, but David felt differently. He had a burning passion to see God's presence restored to its proper place in Jerusalem. He wanted to live under the shadow of God's glory.

The Church has been "playing church" for too long. It is time for someone to stand up and say, "The era of Saul is over!" Saul was a king after the flesh; David was a king after the Spirit. Saul was a king chosen because he stood head and shoulders above everybody else (according to outward appearance and qualifications), and he "appeared" to be the right one. He was named king only because the people pressed God for "second best." Saul quickly lost his God-given mandate to rule by choosing to please men by his actions instead of God. There is no room for a politician in the stewardship of God. We have only one "public" to please as children of God, and that is the audience of One who made us for His own pleasure.

David, on the other hand, was God's chosen king, a man who had been groomed all his life through intimate relationship. When God ripped the kingdom out of Saul's hand to put it into David's hand,[2] David said in essence through his actions, "We're not going to pursue God in the fleshly ways any longer." When people like you and me stand up and declare our intentions as God chasers, the Church will never be the same again.

Looks Don't Matter Anymore

There are steepled buildings all over North America, but no matter what the sign on their manicured front lawns say, God is quite unwelcome in those places. Why? Because their programs, their dignity, and their respectability among men are more important than the presence of God. Yet God is beginning to rain down His grace and mercy, and, a little bit at a time, His thirsty people are changing. No longer do they care about the imposing appearance of a building or the professional look of a man-made program—they are hunting for God. They want the *ark* of God's presence back in the Church.

You may be in the same place I am in today. I've been in too many ark-less church services. I've endured too many powerless choir songs. I'm even tired of my own ministry! I have preached too many sermons that may have been anointed but didn't usher in the very presence of the One we all long for. Maybe I was doing the best I knew how to do, but all I could do was muster up a faint scent of Him, the merest hint of something immeasurably better and more powerful.

All I could do under the anointing was make some smoke on the wrong side of the veil when what we really longed to do was slip underneath and behold His glory behind the veil. I'm thankful for the anointing, but now I know that God has even more for us—*Himself*. I struggled and worked at the ministry for decades, but now I've discovered that when the weighty presence of God comes in, everything I can do pales in comparison. When God comes on the scene in His manifested presence, everything—sinners and saints, rich and poor, wise and foolish, young and old alike—*everything* falls down in awe of His glory. We must move from asking for anointing to pursuing His manifest presence, the *glory*. Anointing empowers the flesh—you preach or sing better. "Glory" flattens flesh! Go for the glory!

David remembered his intimate fellowship with God in his father's fields. He remembered his supernatural encounters with the Lord as a lowly young shepherd facing lions, bears, and the mightiest warrior of Philistia. Now many years later, as the newly crowned king of both Judah and Israel, David made the first move to fulfill his dream:

> *Then* [David] *said to the whole assembly of Israel, "If you approve, and if the Lord our God opens a way,* let us send to our kinsmen who have stayed behind in all the districts of Israel, and also to the priests and Levites in the cities and towns where they have common lands, bidding them join us. Let us fetch the Ark of our God, *for while Saul lived we never resorted to it"* (1 Chronicles 13:2-3 Revised English Bible[3]).

The "Sauls" and the flesh have tried to do it long enough. Thank God for pastors and churches who are hungry enough for the presence of God to lay everything else aside and say, "We might have a nice building, we might have a tabernacle, but *we need Him!*" Many times Israel had all the trappings of God but didn't have *Him*. The Jews of Jesus' day had the tabernacle, they performed every ritual sacrifice to perfection, they went through all the motions of the law, and they kept the Levitical priesthood working round the clock—but *the ark of the covenant was gone.* I sometimes wonder if the split veil was also to reveal the emptiness of religion gone awry. The rip revealed that the Holy of Holies was empty. (They couldn't fathom that the "Holy of Holies" of the Father had just been ripped by a Roman spear on a hill not far away from the temple.) All the activity took place outside the veil, while behind the veil there was only empty silence. Sometimes you must acknowledge that something is missing and take a trip to get the "ark." *Pharisees never like to admit that they possess less than everything.*

> *So David gathered all Israel together...to bring the ark of God from Kirjathjearim.*
> *And David went up...to bring up thence the ark of God the Lord, that dwelleth between the cherubims, whose name is called on it* (1 Chronicles 13:5-6).

In David's day, if you wanted the glory of God then you had to go to the ark of the covenant. The ark was still at Abinadab's house in Kirjathjearim, where it was left by the stunned Israelites from Bethshemesh after more than 50,000 of them had died. They were killed because they looked upon the sacred ark of God's presence as a common box. They presumed to open the ark of God's presence and look inside as if it were nothing more than a pretty toy box. Twenty years later, David made a 15-mile pilgrimage to find the missing glory:

> *And they set the ark of God upon a new cart, and brought it out of the house of Abinadab that was in*

Gibeah: and Uzzah and Ahio, the sons of Abinadab, drave the new cart.

And they brought it out of the house of Abinadab which was at Gibeah, accompanying the ark of God: and Ahio went before the ark.

And David and all the house of Israel played before the Lord on all manner of instruments made of fir wood, even on harps, and on psalteries, and on timbrels, and on cornets, and on cymbals.

And when they came to Nachon's threshingfloor, Uzzah put forth his hand to the ark of God, and took hold of it; for the oxen shook it.

And the anger of the Lord was kindled against Uzzah; and God smote him there for his error; and there he died by the ark of God.

And David was displeased, because the Lord had made a breach upon Uzzah: and he called the name of the place Perezuzzah to this day.

*And David was afraid of the Lord that day, and said, **How shall the ark of the Lord come to me?***

So David would not remove the ark of the Lord unto him into the city of David: but David carried it aside into the house of Obededom the Gittite (2 Samuel 6:3-10).

David and his crew were trying to handle the holy presence and glory of God with human hands. How do you handle the holiness and glory of God? God will only let you do things your way just so far. I've heard it said that David's caravan "hit a *bump in the road* at the threshing floor." Who put that "bump" in the road? That would be like God! He still has a way of putting speed bumps in the middle of the highway of man's reasoning. They force us to slow down and ask, "Is this the right thing?"

The Bump in the Road

*D*avid's problems came when he and his troupe tried to continue on as normal past God's speed bump. The Lord never intended for His glory to creak along on the back of man's mechanisms, vehicles, or programs. He has always ordained for His glory to be transported by sanctified or set apart holy human vessels who reverence and respect His holiness.

Abinadab's sons had spent up to 20 years around the ark. To them, it was an ornate but ordinary box or chest. They were probably honored when they were chosen to drive the cart carrying the ark, but neither one of those young men was prepared, and they didn't know about the ancient warnings concerning God's holiness. When David's procession came to God's holy shaking place in the road, the oxen stumbled and Uzzah reached out to steady the ark. Uzzah's name literally means "strength, boldness, majesty, security."[4] The presence of God never needs the assistance or guidance of man's strength to hold its rightful place. Nor will God ever allow the arm of flesh to glory in His presence without tasting death.

God's glory "broke out" on the flesh that drew near to it in a living state and Uzzah was instantly killed. *Only dead men can see God's face*, and only repentant dead flesh can touch His glory.

I don't think any of us have seen the Church function on the order of the church at Jerusalem in the Book of Acts. The deaths of Ananias and Sapphira for lying to God described in Acts 5:1-11 should be reexamined by the Church today. That same Spirit is beginning to visit the Church today, and His standards of holiness have not changed. When the glory of God descended on that young church, it brought fear on the people, but it also brought

God's miracle-working power through signs and wonders, causing many to be added to the church (Acts 5:11-16). Why? Because the leaders who were submitted to God flowed in His power and authority. (You have nothing to fear from "Dad" if you haven't done anything bad while "Dad" was gone!)

As soon as God's presence fell on us in small measures of glory, we began asking ourselves the same questions David must have asked himself when he saw how serious it was to be the stewards entrusted with God's manifest presence. We began to ask ourselves, "Should we really be the ones to take care of this sacred Presence?" I distinctly remember saying over and over, "Why me, Lord?" David, the psalmist of the hills and the warrior of God, had suddenly discovered another facet of God's character that he had never seen before. Evidently no one else in Israel had seen this side of God either. Sadly, neither has the Church of today.

David decided to cancel the trip to Jerusalem and pull aside to leave the Presence he now feared at the home of Obededom in nearby Gath (formerly a Philistine stronghold). The ark stayed there for three months, and the Lord blessed Obededom, his family, and everything that he owned.

Why did David stumble like the oxen pulling the cart? He was in shock. He had been doing everything he knew to do in the most respectable manner that he knew of. (In fact, David's methods resemble the methods used by the *Philistines* years earlier to transport the ark into Israelite territory according to First Samuel 6:7.) He was dancing at the head of the procession and around the cart along with the rest of the people while many played instruments and sang. He obviously believed that God would be pleased with his efforts that day.

They were a happy little "church" taking the presence of God to the place where it belonged. Then they hit a holy bump in the road at the threshing floor of *Nachon,* a Hebrew word which ironically means "prepared."[5] They were obviously unprepared. When Uzzah casually reached out to steady "God's box" from falling off of man's vehicle, God seemed to say, "Look, I've let you come this far in your own manner; enough is enough. If you really want My presence back in Jerusalem, then you're going to have to do it My way." Then He struck down Uzzah right on the spot and stopped David's parade in its tracks. *God broke out of His box and caused man's plans to fall* that day, and it would take David three months to recover, repent, research, and return for God's glory. The same thing happens today when we encounter God's manifest glory. Too often we reach out in fleshly presumption to stop the God we've carefully contained in a box from falling off of our rickety man-made ministry program or tradition. We shouldn't be surprised when God's glory breaks out of our doctrinal or traditional boxes and shocks us. Something always dies when God's glory encounters living flesh.

David changed his plans and methods because the weightiness of the presence of God suddenly dawned on him. He began to think, *This is no small matter. What are we doing? Am I really the one who should be doing this?*

Do You Want to Pay the Price?

That is exactly where the Church is at this crucial moment in time: We have reached the point in this *move of God* where we are trying to transport the glory back to where it belongs. We've run into the shaking place at God's threshing floor and it is time to ask ourselves, "Are we really the ones? Do we really want to do it? Are we willing to pay the price and obey God's voice at all costs? Are we willing to learn anew how to handle the holy things of God?"

I must warn you that God's glory, His manifest presence, can literally split local church bodies like the "split" body of Uzzah. Many a godly pastor should approach his congregation with kindness and diplomacy to say:

> "If you're not serious about seeking God's face, then you might want to find another place. If you're uncomfortable about waiting on the presence of God and experiencing the weightiness of God's glory; if you are uncomfortable with the strange and unusual manifestations that sometimes accompany His coming, then you need to find someplace less hungry to stay. We've had church our way long enough. If you want to keep having church 'the way Saul did it' yesterday, if you are content to put God in His familiar box and strap it to your own man-made programs and procedures, then you might need to go somewhere else. I must warn you that the 'bump in the road' just told us that we are not going to do it that way anymore."

It's when you hit that holy bump at the threshing floor of "preparation" that you realize, "This won't work anymore. This is not right anymore." Until you hit that bump, you will probably be perfectly satisfied and at ease with a little dancing, some small harps (that aren't *too* noisy), a few people singing and dancing, and maybe even a few less conservative things from time to time. But once you decide to return God's glory to its proper place, you are destined to hit a holy bump when God's glory appears and slays some flesh right in front of everybody. True repentance is an

149

awesome flesh-death sight to behold... too much for some to stomach.

That day when I leaned over to whisper to the pastor in fear and trembling, "*God could have killed you!*" we both knew we had reached the point of the bump in the road. God said, "Are you serious about Me coming? Do you really want Me to? Then you're going to have to do it My way."

No one but God knows how the Israelites handled the ark when they first loaded it onto the new cart at Abinadab's house, but we do know they handled it differently after Uzzah's death. We can be sure about one thing: *Nobody touched it.* They had a new respect for God's glory that wouldn't wear off for a lifetime. They probably said, "Good luck, Obed. You should probably know that we have to bury a man today because he touched that thing when we hit a bump in the road. You'd better be careful, Obededom."

David wondered, "I don't know if I really want that ark in Jerusalem. It might kill us all." The only problem was that for the next three months, David kept hearing reports about God's blessings on Obededom. According to the Bible, Obededom's house was so blessed that everything he touched was blessed too! That seemed to include everything he owned, all his family members, and even his second cousins and farm animals were doing better. Money was flowing in and everybody was healthy. When David checked with Obededom, he said:

> "Yeah, you've heard right."
> "Well, what have you done?"
> "I know we sure haven't touched that thing; I won't let the kids get close to it. But ever since you dumped that box off on my front porch, it's just like that thing is emanating riches, power, and authority. When I walk into town, things

happen that I didn't even have anything to do with."

David quickly reconsidered his official position on the ark. It had suddenly dawned on him what the presence and the glory of God could mean to a *nation* if it brought blessing to even a lowly farmer's family. Then he said, "I've got to get that ark back where it belongs. I'm going to get it to Jerusalem." When David put the ark on the new cart the first time around, he had "all of Israel" with him thinking, *Wow, God will be pleased with the way we did this. Look at all the thousands of guys gathered around the ark playing instruments and dancing.*

Since no one bothered to ask God for His opinion about it all, He had to pull the plug on the party. "No more, not one step further. I'm shaking things up! You've hit the holy bump on the threshing floor and this is where the flesh gets off. This is as far as you go *doing it your way.* If you really want My presence to be where it belongs, then from here on out you do things *My way.*"

The second time around, David did what he should have done the first time. He studied the history of past moves of God in the Word. How did they move the ark of the covenant from one place to another in Moses' day? He rediscovered the true purpose and function of the Levites and the Aaronic priests, and he noticed for the first time that wooden staves were meant to be put through the mysterious rings on the side of the ark. "Oh, so *that's* what those rings are for." It's amazing that God got "bent out of shape" over two sticks!

Don't Take God for Granted

A lot of hungry church leaders today are reading everything they can find about past moves of God. Why? Because we are at the holy bump in the threshing floor. We somehow sense that if we really want the holiness of God and the fullness of His glory to dwell in our midst, then we need to find out how to properly handle the holy, God's glory. We know that this is where the flesh has to fall off, but what is God's way to do it? Our hunger is too deep for one meal to satisfy us. We are after more than His visitation. We want God's visitation to become a *habitation*. We want His *kabod*, not "Ichabod." We want His *present* presence to be here.

We are in the same situation as King David. Our greatest danger at this point is for *the sacred things to become common*. The ark of the covenant was housed in Abinadab's home for a long time, but God's presence was only there in a limited fashion. Some writers think Uzzah grew up around the ark of the covenant as a kid. Perhaps he played on it, sat on it, or swung his feet from the sides, and generally didn't think anything about it. If this is true, it was because God was there in a limited fashion.

However, when you start moving God's glory back to the place where it belongs, His "felt" or manifested presence and power will begin to be restored with every step back to His divine order. (Could the stumbling have come from the additional "weight" of the glory, the *kabod*, being restored to the ark?) You will no longer be able to get away with things that you used to take for granted. If we're not careful, we can allow sacred things to become so common that we begin to think like Uzzah: *I can touch it, see? I grew up with it; it's harmless*. We're going to touch God's glory one time too many.

Never take God's holy presence for granted, and never assume that if no one is crying, shaking, manifesting odd movements, or prophesying away, then God isn't at work. Be careful when you stifle a yawn of boredom and complacency. Many of the great saints in historic denominations and churches knew that God doesn't always have to manifest Himself in things seen by the eye of the flesh. They would solemnly warn all of us, "Don't come in here looking for sensationalism. Come looking for God and you will find Him."

We need to live with a new awareness of His constant presence. I want to be careful so it won't become so common to me that I begin to think I can casually reach out and touch His holiness with my flesh at any point. I want *Him* at any cost, and I will not let sacred things become common to me. If you are committed to participate in the visitation and habitation of God, then pray this with me:

> "Lord God, I am here to meet with You, and
> I am learning how to handle the holy things of
> Your presence. Have mercy on me, Lord Jesus."

One of the first things God does when He "turns on the power" in His Church is to bring back a respect for that power. Any electrician or experienced "do-it-yourselfer" will tell you that before they wire a house, they always turn off the power first. Why? Most will admit it is because they have *touched the power* before! What did they gain from the experience? They received a deep and personal respect for the power of electricity and its effect on unprotected flesh.

Before God brings His power into the earth, in His mercy He first restores our respect and awe for His glory and the things that are holy. We need to regain a deep and personal respect for the power of God's glory on unrepentant flesh. It's not that we shouldn't come near it, "use" it, or dwell in it. Just as an electrician is able to work around crackling 220-volt power lines with safety once he learns to respect the power of electricity, David and the Israelites learned how to honor and "handle" or steward God's glory manifested in the ark of the covenant. In fact, they even took the ark into battle with them later on. God is calling you and me to carry His presence "into battle" with us every day as "living arks" or tabernacles of the Most High God. He wants us to dwell with Him in intimate communion—but first the flesh must die.

The anointing and power of God's presence are going to come upon us so strongly that His presence will literally go before us into our offices, plants, prisons, and shopping malls. Because this great revival is based on His glory and presence and not on the works of man, it cannot be contained within the four walls of churches. God's glory must flow out to the world.

There is another point to notice in David's second attempt to move God's glory into its proper place. When he recalled the Levites and the descendants of Aaron to the priestly duties as stewards of the ark, he gave them a solemn warning that applies to every high priest in the Kingdom of God today:

> *And said unto them, Ye are the chief of the fathers of the Levites: **sanctify yourselves**, both ye and your brethren, that ye may bring up the ark of the Lord God of Israel unto the place that I have prepared for it.*
>
> *For because ye did it not at the first, the Lord our God made a breach upon us, for that **we sought Him not after the due order*** (1 Chronicles 15:12-13).

The Hebrew word translated as "sanctify" is *qadash*, and it means to "separate" or "make holy."[6] In other words, we have to become holy like He is. Do you know how David emphasized the importance of sanctification to those men? I think he said, "I want to show you the tombstone of a guy who wasn't sanctified. You're about to carry the same ark of the covenant that did this to him, so you had better go through a cleansing ceremony right now. You better cleanse yourself." I know that the first man to thrust a stave through the rings counted himself as dead. Only "dead men walking" can host God's holiness.

Worth More Than a Coke

*T*his move of God taking place across the earth has often been marked by night after night of cleansing in repentance. If we allow God to take us through the *complete* process of repentance and brokenness without hindering or quenching His Spirit, then when the *kabod*, the weighty presence of God, comes among us and upon us, then we will be able to carry it without fear because we will be walking in the purity of Jesus and our flesh will be dead, covered by the blood of the Lamb.

The old-timers in the Pentecostal movement used to do some things that I made fun of as a young man. I have an aunt who "gave up drinking Coke" when she was seeking the presence of God in her life. She really enjoyed drinking Coca-Cola, but she prayed, "God, if You will visit me, I'll *never drink another one*." God took her at her word.

I used to laugh about it as a kid and tease her as I waved a Coke in front of her. "Here, you want a Coke?" She would just laugh and say, "No, I don't want a Coke." Even then that laugh of hers always left me feeling like *she knew something I didn't*. Now, ever since the first day of God's manifested presence showing up in Houston, I can say, "I understand now, Auntie. I understand." *Nothing is worth holding on to so hard that you can't hold Him.*

⥱ Notes from those on the chase ⥱

My name is Emeka N. and I live in Port-Harcourt, Rivers State, Nigeria. I was introduced to your book, **The God Chasers,** *when you were on Benny Hinn's program on the TBN satellite network some time ago when he reviewed the book* **The God Chasers.** *That encounter so touched me that I went around all the Christian bookstores in town until I bought a copy of* **The God Chasers.** *After reading the first two chapters of the book, questions that I'd been asking myself were answered.*

I thank God for raising up somebody with this message in these times that teaches to go all-out and chase God just like David in the Bible. These are the kind of people God is looking for. We have been playing church and trying to impress man in our churches so much that we have ended up driving people out of church. Truly, as you said, we come into church to find God but most of our pastors end up showing themselves to us instead of introducing God to us.

I had been so disturbed about it that for a time I thought I was different from others because I came out of services more empty than full. After discovering Proverbs 18:1 and some other verses of Scripture, I realized that my spiritual growth depended on me and not any pastor. So I started reading the Bible and buying books to fill my hunger, which was much until I discovered your book, which showed me that somebody else was going through the same things I was going through.

...I would like to know about other books you have written so I can read them, because I truly desire God and I'm hot on His heels. You have started a big fire/hunger for God in me, and I'm on the trail again chasing after Him. I know if I run fast and sure, I'll discover not only His track, but I also will get very, very close to Him.

—Emeka N.

*My name is Jovian M. I'm 19 and almost three years old in Jesus...I just wanted to testify that I picked up the book, **The God Chasers**, after having it suggested to me, and wow, what a book. It was right up my alley! I love books that speak of seeking God and worshiping Him and learning how to worship Him and talk about His presence and the like. And glory...this book was like a ton of manna falling on my head. It was so hard and solid...just some really powerful material—and material that the Body of Christ needs to have placed in itself.*

I must say, it has already begun to change the way I worship and the way I behave in church, but I'm sure that its long-term effects won't be seen until later. It's like, I'm having all this info planted in me, and when I can apply it all, something is going to explode. I just want to continue to learn and grow and mature in Christ.

I really thank God for this book and the two others that followed it, which hit me hard as well, and I pray that it reaches one million people a million times more. I have to say that this book messed me up and left me crippled at times. That's such a great feeling, to be broken and have God replace self. Then we can walk at His Word.

It added a keg of fuel within me, and I know when God reveals more to me and helps me understand it all, something is going to get off...and that something will do damage to the kingdom of darkness.

—Jovian M.

*I have read your book, **The God Chasers**, eight times. I couldn't put it down. I pastor First Assembly in Arkansas and had the opportunity to bring eight people from our church to your God Chasers Rally in Springdale,*

Arkansas...Needless to say, it changed our lives. Our Sunday morning service was filled with His presence as our people responded with true praise and worship to God. I watched as people who had never shown any signs of wanting more of God, came forward...

—K.

Ask Some Questions

1. How did the Israelites treat the Ark without the respect it deserved?

   In what way are we treating the holy things of God without due respect?

2. How did David first learn from his mistakes? What did he do differently the second time?

   How can we follow David's example and learn from history and our mistakes?

3. Have you ever hit a divine "bump in the road"? Did you think it was "divine" at the time?

   What speed bumps loom ahead in your road?

Endnotes

1. A.W. Tozer is one of my favorite authors. I recommend you read *Tozer on Worship and Entertainment: Selected Excerpts*, compiled by James L. Snyder (Camp Hill, PA: Christian Publications, 1997).

2. See 1 Sam. 28:17.

3. *Revised English Bible* [a revision of *The New English Bible*] (Oxford and Cambridge, England: Oxford University Press and Cambridge University Press, 1989).

4. James Strong, *Strong's Exhaustive Concordance of the Bible* (Peabody, MA: Hendrickson Publishers, n.d.), **Uzzah** (#H5798, #H5797). Definition adapted from the original definition.

5. *Strong's*, **Nacon** (#H5225).

6. *Strong's*, **qadash** (#H6942).

Chapter 7

HE'S DONE IT BEFORE; HE CAN DO IT AGAIN

Send the rain, Lord!

We want God to change the world. But He cannot change the world until He can change us. In our present state we are in no position to *affect* anything. But if we will submit to the Master Potter, He will make us—all of us—into what He needs us to be. He may remake the vessel of our flesh many times, but if we will submit to the Potter's touch, He can turn us into vessels of honor, power, and life. After all, wasn't He the One who turned unlearned fishermen into world-changers and hated tax collectors into fearless revivalists? *If He did it once, He can do it again!*

I want to break the standard writing "rules" for Christian books and ask you to pray a prayer with me right now, as you read the first page of this chapter. This book was written to help usher God's presence into your life and church family. It may sound silly, but I want you to put your hand on your heart and pray this "prayer of the clay" with me right now:

"Father, we thank You for Your presence. Lord, the air is just pregnant with possibility and we sense Your nearness. But we must say that You are not near enough. Come, Holy Spirit. If not now, when? If not us, who? And if not here, where? Just tell us, Lord, and we'll go; we will pursue Your presence because we want You, Lord. Your presence is what we are after and nothing less will do."

Something is happening in the Body of Christ. More and more of us are unwilling to play the old religious games. Something like a warrior spirit is rising up within us, an urge to conquer territory in the name of the Eternal One. I know that in my life, I've received a mandate from the Lord to pour my life into key cities where I sense God intends to pour out His Spirit in the days ahead.

I'm shopping for places where God is "breaking out." I've already described how God "broke out" in the city of Houston (and I mention it simply because I was privileged to be present when God came on the scene). I have felt led to participate in continual meetings for more than a year in some places, and incredible things are happening. We still have a long way to go, but in each city we did something that has deep spiritual significance for this move of God. I want to see a contagious outbreak of God like was seen with Finney, Edwards, Roberts, and company, where whole regions are swept into the Kingdom.

I'm After Entire Cities

I am after cities; I'm not interested in just preaching in churches to Christian people. I'm

162

after entire cities occupied by people who don't know Jesus. Once while preaching at a conference with Frank Damazio in Portland, Oregon, I heard him mention something that instantly captured my attention. He said that a number of pastors in the Portland area had united together to drive some stakes in the ground at strategic places around the perimeter of their region and the city and at every major intersection. The process took them hours because they also prayed over those stakes, as they were physical symbols marking a spiritual declaration and demarcation line.

I felt the stirring of the Holy Spirit so I said, "Frank, if you'll provide the stakes, then I will go to cities I feel called to and help the pastors stake out that territory for God." Then I began to ask God in prayer, "Lord, give me some precedent so I can understand what You are doing here. Then I'll know why You have pressed this into my heart."

Ironically, this stirring of the Lord came upon me later in California, and I was reminded that California was the site of the great "gold rush." Whenever would-be gold prospectors found a spot of ground where they thought there might be some gold, they would "stake a claim." Some plots of property are just more valuable than others because of what is *in the ground.* If you wanted to claim a plot of ground in those days, then you would "stake" it by driving a stake into the earth. That stake would bear your name and a rough description of the area you were claiming. Later the land would be formally surveyed, but until then, a claim stake was as good as a land deed in a court of law back in those days. If anybody disputed your claim, you could go to that undisturbed plot of ground and dig up your stake bearing your name and the rough dimensions of the claim and say, "See, I've claimed it according to law. I am in the process of possession and occupation, but this claim stake is proof that the land is already mine by law."

Pastors and congregations who have put down roots in a city or region have a "legal right" under God to claim their cities for the King by "staking" out the territory. In the past, too many of us have been content to keep our faith contained within the four walls of our meeting halls and church buildings. Now God is calling us to extend our faith beyond to the boundaries of our cities and nation. In effect, we are literally expanding the "walls" of our spiritual churches when we stake out our cities. It forces us to see ourselves as "the Church" in the city, one people under God comprised of many congregations according to the first century pattern of the "city-church."

We actually made wooden stakes with four sides bearing the words, "Renewal, Revival, Reconciliation," along with supporting Scriptures. A hole was drilled down the middle of the stake and a rolled-up written proclamation was inserted in it. Altogether, there are about 20 Bible verses in the stakes and proclamation, but one of them is Isaiah 62, which says:

> *Behold, the Lord hath proclaimed unto the end of the world, Say ye to the daughter of Zion, Behold, thy salvation cometh; behold, His reward is with Him, and His work before Him.*
> *And they shall call them, The holy people, The redeemed of the Lord: and thou shalt be called, Sought out, A city not forsaken* (Isaiah 62:11-12).

Repent, Request, and Resist

The written proclamation contained in every stake driven into the ground of these cities contains this declaration made by God's lawful representatives of that city:

"On the basis of scripture, I stand for leaders of this city, and I stand as a representative for other city pastors who desire to do three things: repent, request, and resist.

"We **repent**, we ask the Lord to forgive us for the sins that have taken place in this state and this region, specifically this city. We ask for forgiveness of the sins of political corruption, racial prejudice, moral perversions, witchcraft, occult, and idolatry. We pray the blood of Jesus to cleanse our hands from the shedding of innocent blood. We ask forgiveness for divisions in the church, forgiveness for pride, forgiveness for the sins of the tongue, anything that has hurt the cause of Christ. We repent and humble ourselves to ask for mercy to be poured out on our land, our community, and our churches.

"We **request**, we ask for God's kingdom to come, and His will to be done in this city. We ask in the Name of Jesus for an outpouring of grace and mercy and fire, for true spiritual revival to come and cover the community, causing a turning back to God, a cleansing, and a brokenness, and a humility. We ask for the destiny of this city not to be aborted. We ask that you visit this city and our churches, and our homes. Do not pass this city by. We ask for a restoration of the foundations of righteousness to this city.

"We also **resist**, on the basis of my submission to God; by faith I resist the devil and his works, all forces, and all powers of evil that have taken hold of the city. We resist the spirit of wickedness that has established strongholds in this city, the dark places, the hidden works of

165

darkness, the mystery places where the enemy has set up encampments. We call on the name of the Lord to destroy all spiritual strong holds, we proclaim this day that this city, especially this region, is now under the power and ownership of the Holy Spirit. All other spirits are hereby given notice, and evicted from this property by the power of the Name of Jesus. Today we stand in the gap and build a hedge of protection around this city."[1]

Before you ever purchase property in the natural, you need to have it surveyed or staked, and you need to determine *if you are willing to pay the price* to possess the land. When we stake our cities as God's people, we are in effect declaring open war on satan's kingdom. Our acts are bold acts of outright aggression without apology or hesitation. We're telling the devil, "We have declared this before God, and now we are telling you, 'We will take the city!' "[2]

A word of the Lord has come to me about "old wells" that applies directly to cities as well as to older mainline denominations and churches. God is going to redig or uncap the old wells *first*, before the newer artesian wells break open. Genesis chapter 26 tells us that Isaac had his men redig the wells that his father, Abraham, had originally dug many years before in the Valley of Gerar. Although his father's enemies had filled in the wells after Abraham's death, Isaac still called them by their original names. He found so much water there that he constantly battled with Philistine raiders and finally moved to Beersheba, or "the well of the oath." It was here that Jacob encountered the living God and discovered his true birthright in God's plan.[3]

In this day, God is uncapping some of the ancient wells of revival. These are places where His glory is like a standing pool of water. People have to *come to the well* to get satisfied, and that is by God's design.

Before God brings forth the new wells, He will redig the old wells.[4] In the year before I began working on this book, the Lord spoke to my spirit and said, "I am going to re-visit the places of historical revival to give My people another chance. I will call them to dig out the debris from the old wells so that the starting of the new revival will be upon the foundations of the old revival."

In simple terms, before the real revival breaks out in the malls, it will have to break out in our church altars. Then the back pews. Then is when the glory of the Lord can flow underneath the threshold of the door and out into the streets in fulfillment of the prophecy in Ezekiel 47:

> *Afterward he brought me again unto the door of the house; and, behold, **waters issued out from under the threshold of the house** eastward: for the forefront of the house stood toward the east, and the waters came down from under from the right side of the house, at the south side of the altar.*
> *Then brought he me out of the way of the gate northward, and led me about the way without unto the utter gate by the way that looketh eastward; and, behold, there ran out waters on the right side.*
> *And when the man that had the line in his hand went forth eastward, he measured a thousand cubits, and he brought me through the waters; **the waters were to the ankles.***
> *Again he measured a thousand, and brought me through the waters; **the waters were to the knees.***
> *Again he measured a thousand, and brought me through; **the waters were to the loins.***

167

Afterward he measured a thousand; and it was a river that I could not pass over: for the waters were risen, waters to swim in, a river that could not be passed over.

And it shall come to pass, that every thing that liveth, which moveth, whithersoever the rivers shall come, shall live: and there shall be a very great multitude of fish, because these waters shall come thither: for they shall be healed; and every thing shall live whither the river cometh.

And by the river upon the bank thereof, on this side and on that side, shall grow all trees for meat, whose leaf shall not fade, neither shall the fruit thereof be consumed: it shall bring forth new fruit according to his months, because their waters they issued out of the sanctuary: and the fruit thereof shall be for meat, and the leaf thereof for medicine (Ezekiel 47:1-5,9,12).

Isn't it ironic that the river of God's presence flowing from His sanctuary actually grew *deeper* the further the prophet walked? Finally Ezekiel ended up in water that was over his head and he couldn't touch bottom. He was out of control. I am after an "out-of-control" revival! Its shallowest point should be at the "church" building!

The Next Wave of Glory

I believe that some cities are old wells of God's anointing—places of historical revival. God is calling pastors and congregations in those cities to redig those wells. Unfortunately, digging the debris out of an old well is not a pleasant task. When a pastor friend of mine bought some property in India, he was told that there was an old well on the property. It wasn't a common "vertical" well; it was slanted horizontally into the side of a mountain.

As the ministry workers began to dig out the debris, they found old machinery, discarded furniture, and mounds of old trash among high stands of overgrown weeds and rushes. They found something else too: They encountered hundreds of cobras in that abandoned well, and they had to be removed. My friend told me, "We got that old well all cleaned out and went to bed. When we got up the next morning, we hoped and expected to find a pool of stagnant water waiting for us. But we discovered that the water in the well had begun to bubble up and was flowing so strongly again that it had created a stream overnight!"

The next wave will come as God uncaps the artesian wells of His glory! Many of the wells in the deserts of the Middle East are "standing pool wells." There is enough water seeping up into the natural holding tank of the earth to keep it filled most of the time, even in the desert heat. Almost every living thing in the desert ecosystem makes its way to the oasis or standing pool well for the water of life. God has uncapped abundant standing pools of His presence that have brought life to millions of thirsty believers and unsaved people over the last few years. But they must travel to the well. There is forgotten power in pilgrimage.

Now He is about to release the next stage or wave of His anointing, and it will be unlike the old standing pool wells in that these new wells will be *artesian wells* that will explode with great force. According to *Webster's Ninth New Collegiate Dictionary*, an "artesian well" is "a well made by boring into the earth until water is reached *which from internal pressure flows up like a fountain; a deep-bored well*."[5] This new wave or level of God's glory will come solely from the "deep-bored" people of God's presence. It will explode into our world with such force that His life-giving presence will push beyond every barrier and obstacle to flow into the thirsty streets of our cities and nations. This is how His glory will "cover the whole earth" (see Is. 6:3; Hab. 2:14). Fountains of the deep will break open!

You don't have to go to the waters of an artesian well; *the water goes to you!* Given the fact that water always seeks the lowest level and the path of least resistance, it is easy to see why Jesus, the "brightness of [the Father's] glory, and the express image of His person" (Heb. 1:3a), said, "...the poor have the gospel preached to them" (Mt. 11:5). God's glory always seeks to fill the void in the lives of men. In the days to come, God's glory will emanate from the most confounding places and individuals, and it will begin to flow and fill the lowest and most open of people. And He alone will receive the glory.

The Lord spoke to me clearly about His glory during a rare downpour in Southern California. I was born and raised in Louisiana where we are accustomed to seeing days of rain. There were many times when it would rain continuously for days and nights and no one would think anything about it. But when it rains in Southern California, people take notice. On this particular day, something strange was going on. California was getting a "Louisiana-style" thunderstorm. It was almost a sub-tropical downpour. Back home, people prepare for rain because they are used to it. They build ditches, culverts, and storm sewers, so they are ready for the rain when it comes.

The Los Angeles area, however, is not accustomed to that much rain. I happened to be in a coffee shop when it began. After 20 minutes had passed, I realized it wasn't going to stop so I went out to where I'd parked the car on the street. The water was flowing over the curb and was almost knee-high in the street! I had to wade through it just to get my car out before the water level rose any higher—in just 20 minutes! As I drove away, I said to myself, "They sure don't build storm drains here or something. I don't know where the rain goes at home, but it never gets that deep in the streets that quick."

As I walked through the rain back to my hotel room, I sensed God's presence and just began to weep. As tears mingled with the rain, I sensed the Lord speak to my heart, "Just as they are unprepared for the rain in the natural, so are they unprepared for My rain in the Spirit. And I will come upon them suddenly."

As I prepared for the meeting that night, I listened to the local news and heard the weatherman in Los Angeles say something that struck a prophetic nerve in me. He said, "This is not the last storm. Actually, *they are stacking up* out in the Pacific *like waves,* one against another." Then he added, "They're just going to keep coming," and explained that the source of those waves of rain was El Niño. El Niño in Spanish means "the babe" and is used to refer to the babe of Bethlehem! That weatherman didn't realize that he was prophesying, but he was talking about the "Christ child," the Source of all the waves of glory about to sweep over this planet.

In that moment, something rose up in me and said, "Yes, Lord! Just send wave after wave of Your glory until it has literally flooded everything! May all that is not of You just be washed away downstream." *Rain,* Jesus, *reign!*

Very often the "law of precedent" applies to parallel events in the natural and spiritual realms. I am so hungry for the unleashing of His glory that I can't express its intensity or urgency. So I pray,

> "Lord, just let it rain! Satan is not going to have enough storm sewers to drain off the glory this time. It's going to rise so high that everybody is going to be floated off their feet and out

of control in a mighty wave of the glory of God. Let it rain, Lord!"

Break open the fountains of the deep. Uncap the ancient wells. Reclaim your heritage. Stake the city! The earth is the Lord's!

He's done it before; He can do it again!

Send the rain, Lord.

∽ Notes from those on the chase ∽

*I just had to write and tell you—I am SO thrilled that **The God Chasers** has at last come out in Japanese! It has a message that the Japanese Church is in sore need of hearing.*

I've been getting as many people as possible in my church in Tokyo to buy it and read it—the church's bookstore has sold out three times already! And the response has been great; it has been "challenging" and "eye-opening."

*I pray that God will use **The God Chasers** to ignite a passionate pursuit and hunger for Him in both my church and in Japan.*

—Gordon O.

∽   ∝

I am an Italian pastor who read your wonderful book! Wow! It has really revolutionized my life and ministry. At the point that as a publisher (I am one of the owners of Destiny Image Europe, the new publishing house born out of the American Destiny Image whose owner Don Nori is a close friend of mine), we have printed it in Italian! Many have contacted us saying that the book changed their lives! Many are now God Chasers! Alleluia!

—Pietro E.

Endnotes

1. For further information, contact City Bible Church, 9200 N.E. Fremont, Portland, Oregon, 97220.

2. I felt so compelled by this that I, along with a band of intercessors, went to Bonnie Brae Street in Los Angeles, California, which was the site of the original outbreak that grew so large it had to be moved to Azusa Street. While interceding there on the property, we drove in a stake! Something seemed to break in my heart (and, I hope, in the heavenlies). It felt like we were tapping into an old well! Debris was being removed and repented of. May the waters of Azusa flow again.

3. See Gen. 28:10-16.

4. My good friend, Lou Engle, wrote a book on this subject of "redigging the wells," and in it he deals with all the details of intercessory prayer. See Lou Engle, *Digging the Wells of Revival* (Shippensburg, PA: Destiny Image, 1998).

5. *Webster's Ninth New Collegiate Dictionary* (Springfield, MA: Merriam-Webster, Inc., 1988), 105.

Chapter 8

THE PURPOSE
OF HIS PRESENCE

Divine radiation zones—presence evangelism

ime and again we ask one another, "Why can't I win my friends to the Lord? Why is it that my family members just don't seem interested in God?" The answer may shock you in its bluntness, but the truth often hurts. The reason people who know you aren't interested in your God may be because *you don't have enough of the presence of God in your life.* There is something about God's presence that makes everything else crumble in comparison. Without it, you will be just as pale and lifeless as everybody else around you. No matter what you do, without His presence, you will be "just another somebody" to those around you.

I don't know about you, but I am tired of just being "another somebody" to the lost around me. I have made a decision. I made up my mind and set my heart to declare, "I am going to pursue the presence of God in my life. I am going to get so close to God that when I walk into secular and public places, people will meet Him." They may not know that I'm there, but they will definitely know that *He* is there. I want to be so saturated with God's presence that when I take a seat on a plane, then everyone near me will suddenly feel uncomfortable if they're not right with God—even though I haven't said a word. I'm not wanting to condemn or to convict them; I just want to carry the fragrance of my Father with me.

We understand "program evangelism," where we knock on doors or pass out tracts, or some other program of the church designed to reach the lost. John Wimber helped us to understand "power evangelism," where we mix anointing with the program. In this form of evangelism, we might pray for someone to be healed on the street instead of just witnessing or giving out tracts. But there is a little understood, much underused form of evangelism that I call "presence evangelism." This is where people take note, saying, "They have been with Jesus" (see Acts 4:13). This is when the residue of God on a person creates a *divine radiation zone* of the manifest presence of God, so much so that it affects those around you.[1]

"Shadow healing" would fall into this category. Only it wasn't Peter's shadow that healed anyone;[2] it was the shadow of who Peter walked with that created a zone—a healing zone, or a demon-free zone! The Hebrews believed that the anointing would extend as far as your shadow reached. I believe that the glory will extend as far as His shadow reaches! Cover the earth, Lord!

The Gospel of Mark tells us that immediately after Jesus astounded His disciples by rebuking the sea and the wind during a great storm, they landed in the "country of the Gadarenes" (see Mk. 4:35–5:1). Something happened that day that I pray will happen in our day.

When the sole of Jesus' foot touched the sandy shore of Gadara, one half-mile distant a man possessed of 5,000 demons suddenly was freed from their choking grasp for the first time.[3] "Why? How do you know?" Mark tells us that when the demonized man saw Jesus, he ran to worship Him. Up until that precise moment, the demons had told him where to go and what to do at every other instance. He had no control over his own actions, even when the demons commanded him to cut himself.

So what changed all that? What happened in a moment that wrested that man's mind and physical functions out of the control of 5,000 controlling demon spirits? I'll tell you what happened: *Father stepped back in the house.*

That is what we need today. We need to hear the footfall of God as the sole of His foot touches earth just one time.... When that happens, we won't have to worry about telling little demons to run. We won't even have to scream Scriptures against their prince or practice pulling down demonic strongholds. The purpose of His manifest presence is to "set the captive free," to fulfill Luke 4:18. He wants to finish what He was unable to start in Nazareth when He said, "This day is this scripture fulfilled in your ears" (Lk. 4:21b).

> *"Lord, we want to see You! We are tired of just talking about You like Sunday school children. When are You going to show up, Lord?"*

I pray that an "Isaiah Chapter 6 Visitation" will come to churches in the cities, because all it takes is one footstep of Almighty God in a city to break the chains of decades and centuries of demonic dominion. I pray that we can say with the prophet Isaiah, *"I've seen the Lord."* I'm praying for a corporate breakthrough in the Church, but first I pray that God gives each of us an individual breakthrough in our lives. "Lord, we are not just coming to You to get a blessing. We seek the Blesser." *We need a breakthrough.*

I must warn you that sometimes you will be broken to get a breakthrough. It's just the way it happens. I encourage you to linger and soak in the presence of the Lord at every opportunity. When you draw near to Him, don't hurry and don't rush. Realize that this is (or should be) at the top of your priority list. Let God do a *deep work* in your heart and life. This is the way God creates a "deep-bored" well in your life that will become an artesian well of power and glory in His presence. *The purpose of His presence is to bring deliverance to the captives and victory to the children.*

Nothing Stops a Fight Like Daddy Coming Home!

For centuries we have been fighting spiritual battles with satan and the bad kids from his neighborhood using bold words and sometimes sticks and stones. But it is time for us to cry out to our Father and watch our neighborhood battles take a totally new turn. I tell you with every ounce of faith in my being that if the Father of us all can step down and allow His manifested presence to touch earth *just once*.... If even one tiny tear from His eye can fall in a city like Los Angeles, New York, or Chicago, then the flood of glory it will spawn will bring revival throughout the land as demons flee and sinners fall to their knees! Jesus, help us. Come, Father! Abba Father, Daddy... we need You!

The bottom line is this: If you are really hungry to see Daddy come on the scene, then you have to understand that you must stop seeking His benefits and quit asking for Him to do this and that. We have managed to turn what we erroneously call "church" into a big "bless me club" where we sign up for this blessing and that blessing. I'm not so sure that we need to seek blessings anymore. That's what the Israelites did in all the centuries after they ran from the face of God. We need to seek brokenness and repentance, and say by our actions as well as our words, "God, we want *You*. We don't care if You 'do' anything or not. We are crawling up on the altar. Let Your fire of cleansing fall so we can finally see Your face."

Why would we go through all this? There are at least two reasons I can think of. First of all, the experience of seeing God's glory is life-changing. It is the most habit-forming experience a human being can have, and the only side effect is death to the flesh. The second reason is this: The true purpose of God's presence manifesting in our lives is *evangelism*. If we can carry a residue of God's glory back into our homes and businesses, if we can carry even a faint glow of His lingering presence into lukewarm churches, then we won't have to beg people to come to the Lord in repentance. They will run to the altar when His glory breaks their bondage (and they can't come any other way!). No man comes to the Father any other way except through repentance and salvation through Jesus. Every other so-called way to salvation bears the mark of a thief and a robber.

The Lord knows that we have tried to pave the way for people to come to God through painless, cheap grace and costless revival. But all we wound up with was bargain basement salvations that hardly lasted a week. Why? Because all we gave people was an emotional encounter with man when what they really needed was a death encounter with the glory and presence of God Himself. From here on, our prayer should be:

> "Father, we confess that we want to see change in our lives and in our church so we can bring about change in our city.

> "Give us such a heart and passion after You that we may begin to see Your glory flow out of

us to convict and save the lost. Release Your presence through us as You did through Charles Finney when he walked through factories and saw workers drop to their knees under Your glory and cried out for forgiveness although not one word had been spoken or preached. May the faintest shadow of Your presence in our lives heal the sick and restore the lame we meet in the streets.

"Let Your presence so saturate us that unsaved guests can't step into our homes or be around us with unrepentant hearts. May Your glory bring conviction in their lives that leads to salvation—not because of the words we say, but *because of Your presence and power in our hearts.*"

Honestly, I'm looking for the same kind of revival that they had in the New Hebrides when officials sent for Duncan Campbell, who was conducting nightly revival services in that region. They told the evangelist, "Would you please come to the police station? There are a whole score of people here and we don't know what's wrong with them, but we think you might." (This really happened!)

As the man walked with the officials through the village to the police station at 4:00 in the morning, he said it was like a plague had come on the village. People were weeping and praying behind every haystack and every door. Men were kneeling on the street corners and ladies and children in their nightgowns were huddled around each other in their open doorways weeping and crying.

When the evangelist finally reached the police station, he found scores of people weeping and crying out to the police, "What is wrong?" They didn't even know enough about God to know it was Him! They just knew something was wrong and that they were guilty. The only thing they knew to do was to go to the police station and confess that something was "wrong." What was wrong was that there was sin in their hearts and the conviction of God had come upon them suddenly. When these people began to flood the police station with their confessions of wrong-doing, the police didn't have the answer.

The evangelist stood on the steps of the police station early that morning and preached the simple gospel of repentance and salvation through Jesus Christ and genuine revival came to that place. This is the kind of revival that I'm talking about, the kind that will quickly overwhelm the resources and manpower of every church.

America Is Hungry, But the Bread Is Stale

*F*rankly, we would be totally unable to contain or manage such a harvest of souls in our present state because we don't have enough fresh bread of His presence on our shelves for the hungry masses! It may bother some people that I say that, but I have a problem with our "part-time, gone fishing" church mentality. We touched on this earlier in Chapter 2, "No Bread in the 'House of Bread,' " but it bears repeating until the situation changes. Why is it that on every corner in America's cities we have little convenience stores *that stay open 24 hours a day* just to meet the public's demand for their goods? Meanwhile, most of America's churches supposedly satisfy the nation's hunger for God while operating only two hours a week on Sunday morning! Why isn't the Church staying open every night and day? Aren't we supposed to be offering the Bread of Life to the hungry? Something is terribly wrong, and I don't think it is America's hunger for God. They are hungry all right, but they are smart enough to tell the difference between the stale bread of yesterday's religious experience and the fresh bread of God's genuine presence. Once again we must conclude that the reason the hungry aren't knocking on our doors is because the House of Bread is empty.

It is interesting to note that not one of the 50 largest churches in the world is in the United States. "How can that be? Haven't we sent missionaries around the world for more than 200 years?" The hungry need fresh bread in abundance, not stale crumbs in the carpet from last century's wedding rehearsal dinner.

I have a friend who pastors a church of about 7,000 believers. His church is arguably the best cell-based model church in America, but he told me that he had recently attended a conference overseas and what he discovered there brought tears to his eyes.

He told me, "Tommy, there's something that just really griped me at that conference." He explained that the conference sponsored a workshop for pastors who pastored churches larger than 100,000, and then he said, "I couldn't stand it. I just had to open the door and stick my head into that meeting to see if there was anybody there. The room had about 20 or 30 people in it, and it just griped me that I couldn't go in there." Then with tears in his eyes, he told me, "Then it dawned on me, Tommy. Nobody in that room was an American."

This man has been fairly successful by American standards. He has managed to make a sizable dent on his city of about 400,000, but he wants to do *more*. He isn't a head-counter or a number-chaser who is interested only in competing with other pastors who brag about their Sunday morning attendance figures. He is a God chaser and a soulwinner. His tears weren't tears of jealousy; they were tears of sorrow. If there has ever been a country ripe for revival, it is the United States. It is time for God's people to get desperately hungry after Him, because the fires of revival must first ignite the Church before its flames can spread to the streets.

I am weary of trying to accomplish God's works with the hands of man. What we need for nationwide revival is one thing and one thing only: *We need to have God show up.*

If you want your local high school classes to turn into prayer meetings, then you will need to see God show up. I'm not talking about a theoretical or historical occurrence. There have been times when God's glory has been flowing in His churches so much that His people had to be careful in area restaurants. Simply bowing their heads to pray over their meal, they look up to see waitresses and other customers all around, just weeping uncontrollably and saying, "*What is it* with you people?"

My wife was standing in line to pay for some purchases at a store during God's visitation in Houston when a lady tapped her on the shoulder. She turned around to see who it was to find a total stranger weeping unashamedly. This lady told my wife, "I don't know where you've been, and I don't know what you've got. But my husband is a lawyer and I'm in the middle of a divorce." She began to blurt out her other problems and finally said, "What I'm really saying is, *I need God.*"

My wife looked around and said, "You mean right here?"

She said, "Right here."

My wife just had to ask again, "Well, what about the people in line?"

Suddenly the lady turned to the woman standing in line behind her and said, "Ma'am, is it okay if I pray with this lady right here?"

But that lady was also crying and she said, "Yes, and pray with me too."

There Is No Shortcut

upernatural things like that will happen to you too, but *it only comes one way.* It only comes when the priest and the ministers weep between the porch and the altar and cry out to Jesus Christ, "Spare the people." There is no shortcut to revival or the coming of His presence. God's glory only comes when repentance and brokenness drive you to your knees, because His presence requires purity. Only dead men see God's face. We cannot expect others to repent at that depth if you and I are not willing to continually walk in that level of repentance.

The world is tired of hearing pompous churches preaching popular sermons from behind their elevated pulpits. What right do we have to tell everybody else to repent when there are such glaring problems in our own house? Hypocrisy has never been in style in God's Church, but we've made it the main attraction in "our" version of church. What we need to do is come clean and confess, "Yes, we have some problems. Yes, I have some problems too. But I am repenting of my sin right now. Is there anybody here who wants to join me while I repent?"

I think we will all be surprised at the number of people who will start crawling out from the crevices of society when they see the Church repenting! Once again, it all goes back to our most serious problem—we don't have the bread of His presence. Our churches are filled with "career prodigals" who love their Father's things more than their Father. We come to the family dinner table not to ask for more of the Father, but to beg and persuade Him to give us all the things in His house that He promised are rightfully ours. We open the Book and lick our lips and say, "I want all the gifts, I want the best portion, the full blessing; I want all that belongs to me." Ironically, it was the father's blessing that actually "financed" the prodigal son's trip away from the Father's face! And it was the son's new revelation of his poverty of heart that propelled him back into his Father's arms.

Sometimes we use the very blessings that God gives us to finance our journey away from the centrality of Christ. It's very important that we return back to ground zero, to the ultimate eternal goal of abiding with the Father in intimate communion.

"Lord, put a hunger in our hearts for You, and not just for Your things. We appreciate Your boundless blessings, Father, but we are hungry for You, our Blesser. Come show us the real purpose of Your presence."

❧ Notes from those on the chase ❧

*How can I put into words the effect that Tommy's book,
The God Chasers, had upon my life? I cried all the
way through it because it echoed my heart's desire; it
echoed things I had thought and frustrations I had felt about
myself and about the Church. Yes, it fired something with me
that wants all of God and nothing of me...I want you to
know that the book and your television appearance have
had a big impact on people's lives here [in New Zealand].
The Lord has been speaking to me personally about brokenness, and I know He is doing a deep work in my heart so
I just want more and more of Him and nothing of me. The
Lord certainly used the book **The God Chasers** as a tool to
ignite this desire in me, as He has done for many others.*

—Pamela T.

❧   ❧

*I was in Wal-Mart with my sister, and we saw a copy of
your book. I had told her before that she needed to read
your book, but the Bible bookstore nears us was out of
copies. So she said okay and picked up the book, and we
started on our way around Wal-Mart. She had the book in
her hands, opened it, and started reading it. I immediately
took the book from her and put it in the cart. She asked me,
"Have you lost your mind?" I said, "No, but believe me, you
need to wait until you are at home to read this book." She
said all right, she would wait. Well, she got so busy that she
forgot to read the book at home so she took the book to work
with her. She had not even read two pages when she said she
dropped to her knees beside her desk and started praising
God by crying and lifting her hands. (Luckily her office is
out by itself.) She called me on the telephone to tell me she was
so glad I had not let her read the book in Wal-Mart because*

she would have been laid out in the aisles of Wal-Mart and we would've had to drag her out on her knees just to get her home. Needless to say, she waited until she was at home before she read any more of it.

—Teresa W.

Ask Some Questions

1. How did Peter's shadow affect people? What is a "divine radiation zone"? How might this concept change our thinking about spiritual warfare?

2. Why do our evangelistic efforts, both personal and corporate, often fail? Have you ever tried to evangelize? Do you have any success stories? Why or why not?

   How can you be a "presence evangelist"?

3. What is your favorite fragrance? What is God's favorite fragrance? What attracts God? What attracts people to God?

Endnotes

1. See Heb. 8:11 NIV.

2. See Acts 5:15-16.

3. See Mk. 5:2-6. NOTE: According to W.E. Vine in *Vine's Expository Dictionary of Old and New Testament Words* (Old Tappan, NJ: Fleming H. Revell Co., 1981), 329, a Roman legion in Jesus' day consisted "of upwards of 5,000 men." Many assume there were only 2,000 demons infesting this man because they asked the Lord for permission to invade the bodies of 2,000 swine, but perhaps many of them had to "double up" in their efforts to escape the overpowering pain and terror they felt at the Lord's presence.

Chapter 9

DISMANTLE YOUR GLORY

The burial of man's glory is the birth of God's glory

We have lost the art of adoring the Lord. Our worship gets so cluttered with endless strings of shallow and insincere words that all we do most of the time is "take up space" or "put in prayer time" with a passionless monologue that even God must ignore.

Some of us come to Him clinging to such heavy burdens that we are too frustrated and distracted to see the Father or understand how much He loves us. We need to return to the simplicity of our childhood. Every night that I'm home, I rock my six-year-old daughter to sleep because I love her. Usually she will lay back in my arms, and just before she drifts off to sleep she will remember the problems of the day and say something like, "Daddy, this little boy was mean to me on the playground at school," or "Daddy, I had trouble on my spelling test today." To her these seem like giant problems. I always try to reassure her that everything will be all right in those moments because she is resting in my arms and because I love her. It

191

doesn't matter what anyone said on the playground, and none of her little failures have any power to hurt her because she is in my arms.

Somehow, when I'm able to weave my way through the labyrinth of a six-year-old mind and bring peace to her, I get to enjoy my favorite part of the day. That is when my little girl just lays her head back to look at me with her eyes half open and give me her little smile. The only way I know to describe it is that her face displays sheer adoration and complete security in those moments. She doesn't have to speak; I understand. And then in complete peace she drifts off to sleep, with the smile of safety and trust on her face.

God wants us to do the same thing. Too often we come to Him at the end of our day and "worship" Him with premanufactured mechanics and memorized words. Then, since we are almost totally absorbed with our "playground" offenses and the temporal problems of the day, we lay back in His presence just long enough to say our string of words and deliver our wish list. Then we jump up and run off to continue our frustrated rat-race lives. Often we never seem to find that place of perfect peace.

You Will Have to Face Him

What He wants us to do is just look at Him. Yes, we can tell Him what we feel. We need to tell Him, but He is really waiting to receive our most intimate worship and adoration, the kind that transcends mere words or outward actions. He has set before you an open door, but you will have to "face" Him. You cannot back your way into the door of eternity; you have to walk into it. You will have to stop looking at and listening to other things. He is beckoning to you to "come up hither," and He'll show you the "hereafter" (see Rev. 4:1). That should bring peace to a weary child.

It is dangerous for us to be led by our "number-crunching intellect" because we can over-analyze the causes and the purposes of God. We'll end up like the Pharisees, Sadducees, and scribes of Jesus' day who missed their hour of visitation. I, for one, don't want to do that. Jesus wept over Jerusalem, the symbol of the "home of God's presence" in His day, saying in essence, "You didn't know the hour. *I* came to you and you didn't know. You knew the Word but you didn't know Me" (see Lk. 19:41-44). "He came unto His own, and His own received Him not" (Jn 1:11).

I'm not writing this because you and the many others who will read these words don't know God's Word. On the contrary, I'm saying this because the Lord wants to develop a new level of intimacy with *His people*. He doesn't want us to memorize Bible trivia; He wants us *to know Him*. Paul said that before he was converted to Christ, he understood the law.[1] But after he was converted, he said, "I *know whom* I have believed" (2 Tim. 1:12b). It's one thing to know *about* Him; it's quite another to know Him.

God is calling you to a new level of intimacy. If you dare to answer His call, the Lord will reveal a fresh part of His character. He will pull you so close that you will be breathing the very rarefied air of Heaven. The only way to the place David called "the secret place" is through the door of focused worship, when you lay aside every distraction and focus your body, soul, and spirit upon God.[2] When His presence becomes so strong that you are oblivious to everyone and everything else around you, then healing can come in an encounter with God from which you will never "recover." Your heart will be as permanently disabled with love as Jacob's leg was left with a limp![3]

"My Favorite Services and Yours Are Not the Same"

I was launched on this journey when God spoke to me while in the midst of His presence. He said, "*Son, the services that you consider your favorite services and those I favor are not the same services.*" That is when I realized that we often come to church to "get something" from God, when the Bible tells us over and over again to "minister unto the Lord." Yes, we're involved in ministry all right. Our lives are so filled with ministry to people and the needs of people that we very seldom enter into a place where we can minister to Him. We go away week after week self-gratified, with our itches scratched and our narrow personal needs met. When will we hear God's still small voice saying,

"Would somebody just love *Me*?"

As I said before, the last time I read it, Psalm 103:1 still said, "*Bless the Lord, O my soul*"—but we often practice, "*O my Lord, bless my soul*"!

God's definition of a hero and ours are probably not the same. Consider what He said about the "sinful" woman who broke the alabaster box to anoint the Lord with oil. If Heaven has a hall of fame, then I can tell you someone whose name is going to be right at the top of the list. It is Mary, the woman with the alabaster box. What is so startling about it is that *the disciples were so embarrassed by the woman's actions that they wanted to throw her out*, but Jesus made her actions an eternal monument of selfless worship! Jesus didn't intervene because of Mary's talent, beauty, or religious achievements; He stepped in because of her worship. The disciples said, "To what purpose is this waste?" (Mt. 26:8b). Jesus said, "It's not waste; it's worship." Often dense disciples mislabel things during their political posturing about who sits at the right and who at the left, while Jesus goes "worship hungry." His growling hunger pangs attract an outsider, a "box-breaker," a foot washer! Such worshipers must often ignore the stares and comments of a politically correct church while ministering to Jesus.

He desires our adoration and worship. Heaven's "hall of fame" is filled with the names of obscure people like the one leper who returned to thank God while nine never bothered. It will be filled with the names of people who so touched the heart and mind of God that He says, "I remember you. I know about you. Well done, My good and faithful servant."

Meanwhile in our church services we act like ungrateful children demanding our biblical allowance and blessings. We religiously seek the hand of God, but we know nothing about seeking the face of God and crying out, "I just want You."

Sit in the Lap of the Blesser

*G*od is saying to us, "I have set before thee an open door" (see Rev. 3:7-13). This is one of those seasons when God seems to be throwing open the door of Heaven and saying, "Come in to a new place of intimacy and communion with Me." You don't need to worry about the blessings if you sit in the lap of the Blesser! Just tell Him that you love Him and every blessing you ever imagined will come to you. Seek the Blesser, not the blessing! Seek the Reviver, not revival! Seek His face, not His hands!

Often I see the aisles of churches strewn with people who have climbed into the lap of the Father. I see them hiding their faces underneath benches and pews as they seek the face of God. Something is happening in the Church today, and it has nothing to do with the hype and manipulation of man. Aren't you sick of all that? Aren't you hungry for an encounter with God that's not contaminated by the vain promotions and manipulations of fleshly leaders? Don't you long to have God just introduce Himself to you? You are not alone. There was one woman who marked the road of repentance with her tears and *dismantled her glory* for the Lord.

> *And one of the Pharisees desired Him that He would eat with him. And He went into the Pharisee's house, and sat down to meat.*
>
> *And, behold, a woman in the city, which was a sinner, when she knew that Jesus sat at meat in the Pharisee's house, brought an alabaster box of ointment,*
>
> *And stood at His feet behind Him weeping, and began to wash His feet with tears, and did wipe them with the hairs of her head, and kissed His feet, and anointed them with the ointment.*
>
> *Now when the Pharisee which had bidden Him saw it, he spake within himself, saying, This man, if He were a prophet, would have known who and what manner of woman this is that toucheth Him: for she is a sinner.*
>
> *And Jesus answering said unto him, Simon, I have somewhat to say unto thee. And he saith, Master, say on.*
>
> *There was a certain creditor which had two debtors: the one owed five hundred pence, and the other fifty. And when they had nothing to pay, he frankly forgave them both. Tell Me therefore, which of them will love him most?*
>
> *Simon answered and said, I suppose that he, to whom he forgave most. And He said unto him, Thou hast rightly judged.*

*And He turned to the woman, and said unto Simon,
Seest thou this woman? I entered into thine house,
thou gavest Me no water for My feet: but she hath
washed My feet with tears, and wiped them with the
hairs of her head.*

*Thou gavest Me no kiss: but this woman since the
time I came in hath not ceased to kiss My feet.*

*My head with oil thou didst not anoint: but this
woman hath anointed My feet with ointment.*

*Wherefore I say unto thee, Her sins, which are
many, are forgiven; for she loved much: but to
whom little is forgiven, the same loveth little.*

And He said unto her, Thy sins are forgiven.

*And they that sat at meat with Him began to say
within themselves, Who is this that forgiveth sins
also?*

*And He said to the woman, Thy faith hath saved
thee; go in peace* (Luke 7:36-50).

You may be only a few spiritual inches away from the encounter of a lifetime. If you want to see the face of God, then just follow Mary to the feet of Jesus. Pull out your alabaster box of precious sacrificial praise and worship. You've been holding your treasure back for too long, but there is One here who is worthy of it all. Don't hold anything back!

The Gospels of Matthew and Mark also record this event, and they say that Simon was or had been a leper.[4] Many scholars believe that the account recorded by Dr. Luke is the story of an earlier event, but even so, Simon the Pharisee was *still* a spiritual leper because he was afflicted with the disfiguring sin of hypocrisy. You can always count on some Pharisees with the leprosy of hypocrisy showing up to look with disdain as you rush in to throw your best at the Lord's feet, but who cares? Who knows what problems will be lifted from your shoulders in that moment? Who knows what worries, fears, and anxieties will fade away when you hear Him say, "I accept you."

In God's eyes, we are all lepers in the spirit realm. We need to be those who return to the One who delivered us to offer thanksgiving. God's acceptance means you can ignore all the other voices that say, "I reject you." I don't mean to be rude, but who cares how many other lepers reject you when you have been healed and accepted by the King?

In the Gospels of Matthew and Mark, Mary's harshest critics weren't the Pharisees or Sadducees. The disciples of Jesus were ready to throw her out when Jesus quickly intervened.

> *And Jesus said, **Let her alone**; why trouble ye her? she hath wrought a good work on Me.*
> *She hath done what she could: she is come aforehand to anoint My body to the burying.*
> *Verily I say unto you, Wheresoever this gospel shall be preached throughout the whole world, this also that she hath done shall be spoken of for a memorial of her* (Mark 14:6,8-9).

Are You Always on God's Mind?

Jesus said that this woman who had broken her alabaster box to anoint Him for His burial would never be forgotten wherever the gospel is preached. In other words, *she would always be on God's mind.* Do you want a visitation from God? You will have to make room for Him in your life, no matter how crowded and cluttered it may be at this moment. Sometimes it means your most treasured things may have to be broken to release the fragrance God remembers.

Your brokenness is a sweet-smelling savor to God. He collects every tear that drips from your chin and flows from the corners of your eyes. The Bible says that He has a bottle of memories to hold every tear you've shed.[5] He loves you, so steal away to your secret prayer place and pull out that "alabaster box" of precious anointing you've been saving for such a time as this. Break it at His feet and say, "Jesus, I love You more than anything. I'll give up anything; I'll go anywhere. I just want You, Lord."

Make no mistake, it took humility for Mary to wipe the Lord's feet with her hair. The Bible says a woman's hair is her glory,[6] so Mary used her glory to wipe the feet of Jesus. Middle Eastern women in Jesus' day generally wore their hair "up," and it was often wrapped in a turban or veil when they left their homes for public places. So Mary probably had to unwrap or "dismantle" her hair to wipe the Lord's feet. I don't want to offend anyone, but it is important for us to understand what that really meant to Mary's reputation. Open sandals were the most common footwear, and it was customary for guests to leave their sandals at the door when they entered a house. Since most travelers in Israel shared the main roads with camels, horses, and donkeys, it was impossible to completely avoid the droppings of these animals all day long.

Sandals provided some protection to travelers, and it was unthinkable to wear them into a person's house. Nevertheless, it was certain that the residue of the day's journey (including the odor of the animal droppings) was still deposited on a guest's unprotected feet. For this reason, the dirty job of washing the animal droppings off of everyone's feet was reserved for the most insignificant servant of the household. Any servant who washed a guest's feet was automatically considered the one "who doesn't

count, the unimportant expendable slave," and was openly treated with disdain.

What a picture of humble worship Mary provides.
She dismantled her "glory," her hair, to wipe animal waste
from His feet. Our righteousness and glory are nothing
but filthy rags, fit only to wipe His feet![7]

If you really wanted to dishonor and humiliate a person who entered your home, all you had to do was make
sure that your servants didn't bother to wash his feet. This
was especially true in a Pharisee's house where outward
cleanliness meant everything. Jesus clearly says that when
He entered Simon's house, no one washed His feet (refer
to Luke 7:44). It is almost like Simon wanted Jesus there,
but he didn't want to honor Him. How often do we want
God present in our services but refuse (or ignore) to worship Him as we should?

Are Our Services Tailored for God or Man?

For too long, the Church has asked God to be
"present" but never placed the presence of
God in a position of honor. That means that what we really wanted were His "tricks." We wanted His divine healings, supernatural giftings, and all the miraculous things
He can do; but we really didn't want to honor Him. How
can I say such a thing? Ask yourself if most of our church
services have been custom-tailored to entertain people or
God. Is it more important to us that when an influential
man or woman leaves, he or she says, "Oh, that was *good.*
I enjoyed that"; or that *God* says, "Oh, that was good. I enjoyed that"?

When God entered our services in the past, how often
did we suspend everything we were doing to honor Him?
Or did we consider His arrival as an interruption in our
agenda that was nice, but only in "proper measure." I

wonder if, when Mary broke open the alabaster box containing precious oil of spikenard, she noticed that when her tears fell on our Lord's dusty, unwashed feet, that they made a streak of cleanliness? Did it suddenly dawn upon her what measure of disrespect had been shown toward Jesus, although He was an invited guest in that house? I believe she did, and it broke her heart. Her grief seemed to only turn up the velocity of her tears until they came like a floodgate had been opened. There were so many tears dripping on Jesus' feet that Mary was literally able to use them to wash away the animal dung on His feet!

But what could Mary use to wipe the remaining residue of animal dung from the Lord's feet? She had no honor or authority in that place, so she couldn't ask for a towel. Having nothing else at hand, with no towels provided by servant or master, Mary dismantled her hair and used her glory to wipe Jesus' feet. She took the disdain and public disrespect of that household away from Him and took it upon herself. She removed every evidence of His public rejection with her beautiful hair and took it as her own. *Can you imagine what that did for the heart of God?* Jesus gave us insight into His feelings in that moment when He openly rebuked His host.

> *And He turned to the woman, and said unto Simon, Seest thou this woman? I entered into thine house,* ***thou gavest Me no water for My feet:*** *but she hath washed My feet with tears, and wiped them with the hairs of her head.*
> ***Thou gavest Me no kiss:*** *but this woman since the time I came in hath not ceased to kiss My feet.*
> ***My head with oil thou didst not anoint:*** *but this woman hath anointed My feet with ointment.*
> *Wherefore I say unto thee, Her sins, which are many, are forgiven; for she loved much: but to*

whom little is forgiven, the same loveth little (Luke
7:44-47).

You Must Dismantle Your Glory to Minister to Him

*G*od spoke to me and said, "Mary dismantled her
glory to minister to Me." If all the disciples
were present, there were at least 12 other people in that
room that day, and not one of them attained the intimacy
that she obtained that day. The disciples missed it, even
though they were good people like Peter, James, and John.
Hear me, friend; you can be busy being a disciple and
doing the work, but *miss the worship*! Do you really think
God needs us to do things for Him? Isn't He the Creator
who stepped out on the balcony of Heaven and scooped
out the seven seas with the palms of His hands? Wasn't it
God who pinched the earth to make the mountains? Then
obviously He doesn't need you to "do" anything. What He
wants is your *worship*. Jesus told the woman at the well,
"...true worshippers shall worship the Father in spirit and
in truth: for *the Father seeketh such to worship Him*" (Jn.
4:23).

Like countless numbers of pastors, elders, and dea-
cons in the Church today, the disciples got nervous when
faced with such raw hunger for God and were saying,
"Somebody stop this woman!" But Jesus intervened and
said, "No, finally *somebody is doing something that's right*.
Don't you dare stop her!" The Church doesn't make room
for Marys with alabaster boxes because they make all the
rest of us nervous when they begin to dismantle their
glory, pride, and ego right there "in front of everybody."
(The real problem is that our ego and self-centered glory
stands out like a flashing beacon in the place of humility.)

God is saying to His people, "I will bring you close to
Me *if you will dismantle your glory*." I keep hearing Him

say, "Dismantle your glory; take your ego apart and lay it aside. I don't care who you are, what you feel, or how important you think you are. I want you, but first you must dismantle your glory." Why? Because the burial of man's glory is often the birth of God's glory.

Mary had to get to the point where her passion made her say, "I don't care who sees me do this." You may feel a tugging and drawing in your heart as you read these words. If that is true, then I can almost guarantee that you have learned how to keep a straight face and "keep going" even though you felt like falling at the Lord's feet to ask for mercy and forgiveness. You must let your love break past the shell of "who you pretend you really are." God wants you to openly and boldly let the world know how much you really love Him—even if you have to dismantle your glory right in front of a room full of disdaining disciples. Become a box-breaker! Break the box of "your" precious things and finalize it by a public show of private passion.

God doesn't need your religious service; He wants your worship. And the only worship He can accept is worship that comes from humility. So if you want to see Him, you will have to dismantle your glory and bathe His feet in your tears—no matter what you may find there. (Honestly, isn't that about the only thing your glory is good for? Our righteousness is as a filthy rag in His sight.[8])

An Anointer or the Anointed

We "pedestalize" people whom God has anointed. Whom does God memorialize? Jesus says that what Mary did will "be told for a memorial of her" (Mt. 26:13). We like the anointed; He likes the "anointers"! These are people of His face and feet—oil pourers, tear washers, humble lovers of Him more than lovers of His things.

I believe that Mary actually anointed Jesus *twice*, and was going to anoint Him a third time. First she came as a sinner and anointed His feet, longing to receive forgiveness at any cost in Luke chapter 7. Then she anointed His head at the end of His earthly ministry in Matthew chapter 26 and Mark chapter 14. Jesus Himself said that she did it "for My burial" (Mt. 26:12). Just think of it. He's hanging on the cross, suspended between heaven and earth as though unworthy of both, abandoned by all, breathing His last agonizing breaths.

But what's that He smells...more than the salty smell of blood trickling down His fractured face, stronger than the noise of dice thrown by the soldiers, overpowering the jeers of the Jewish priests? *It's the fragrance of past worship, captured in the locks of His hair...He smells the oil from the alabaster box!* The memory of the worship of an "anointer" strengthens His resolve, and He "finishes" the task at hand.

This same woman who anointed Him in His life witnessed the crucifixion and said, "I can't leave Him unanointed in His death." As she carried yet another compound of precious spices to anoint the Lord's body in the tomb, she found His tomb empty and again felt her heart break with emptiness as she began to bitterly weep and cry. Oh, the love of an anointer! They are willing even to pour anointing over dead dreams!

Jesus had just vacated the tomb and was on His way to sprinkle His shed blood on the mercy seat when He heard her familiar cry. This was potentially the most important task that Jesus ever did, because it was the heavenly fulfillment of the most important task that any earthly high priest ever did in his sanctity and cleanliness. The high priests of Israel had to be very careful to avoid becoming ceremonially defiled, so no woman was allowed to touch them at all. Yet just as Jesus began His ascent on high to sprinkle His blood on the true mercy seat in Heaven, He saw the one who had dismantled her glory to clean His feet, *the anointer.* Perhaps He had one foot on the bottom rung of Jacob's ladder that ascends into Heaven when He abruptly stopped and said, "She's come to do it again. She has come with her precious fragrances and sacrifices of praise, only I am not there to receive it." So He stopped on His way to do the most important task He would ever do and said, "I can't leave her here without letting her know."

You can literally arrest the purposes and plans of God if you are a worshiper. Jesus stopped what He was doing to go to a person who had broken her most precious alabaster box to anoint Him. He stopped when He saw her tears and went to stand behind her. Finally He said, "Mary, Mary."

God Was Arrested By the Cries of a Prostitute

*W*hat made the Son of God do that? Why did the great High Priest of Heaven stop His advance toward the mercy seat for the cries of a former prostitute? I can tell you this: *He only does it for "hall-of-famers."* At first Mary didn't even recognize Him because He had changed. She said, "Where have you put Him? Where have you put the familiar appearance I've grown used to seeing?" She thought the glorified Christ was just the gardener (*sounds like many of us today who often fail to recognize God's glory when it stares us in the face*).

Finally Mary stopped her sobbing enough to really hear His voice as He said, "Mary." His likeness had been changed from mortal to immortal, and His whole countenance had been altered from something of this world to something that was not of this world. He quickly said, "Mary, don't touch Me. I really don't want to go through all that sacrifice on the cross all over again, so don't touch Me. But Mary, I just had to let you know that I am all right. Go tell the disciples."[9] *He had to tell her not to touch Him*; it's as though He knew she would for Him to say this! He also had to be near enough for her to touch Him if she wished to. *It was as if Jesus would have risked being defiled as High Priest for the sake of a worshiper.*[10]

God will whisper His prophetic secrets before they ever come to pass for broken-box worshipers and fragrant anointers. He will turn aside at the height of His glory for people who will dismantle their own glory and ego just to share His shame as their own.

Are You Waiting for the Whisper of God?

*I*n a sense, Jesus was endangering the very purposes of God the Father for a worshiper who would dismantle her glory. That is why He had to be careful to say, "Don't touch Me." What a level of trust He had in her! Have you ever wondered how certain people seem to have a certain attachment to God? For some reason, God just seems to be near them all the time. I can tell you that it isn't because they preach so well, or because they are such stellar singers. No, they know how to dismantle their egos and glory. They lay it all aside just to worship at His feet in brokenness and humility. And it is for these precious few that God Himself will stop His ascent to Heaven just to whisper His secrets into their waiting hearts.

Did you notice that *God* didn't break Mary's alabaster box? *Mary* had to break it. If you want to have that kind of encounter with God, then you will have to "break" yourself. The highest level of worship comes from brokenness, and there are no shortcuts or formulas to help you "reach the top." No one can do it for you; that is something only you can do. But if you do, God will stop just to spend time with you.

If He hears that cracking tinkle when you break your alabaster box of personal treasures; if He notices the rustling sound as you bow to dismantle your own glory; you are going to stop Him in the middle of whatever He's doing, because God cannot pass by a broken and contrite heart.[11] He is going to move Heaven and earth just to come visit with you.

If you want to know why some churches have revival, or why some people have intimacy when multitudes do not; the answer is that *these are people of brokenness*. The breaking of your heart arrests the ears and eyes of God, and it begins when your love for Him supersedes your fear of what others may think. *You can't seek His face and save your "face."* The "end" of your glory, the dismantling, if you please, is the beginning of His glory.

✑ Notes from those on the chase ✑

*I am a new Christian who is e-mailing you from a little town of Labrador City, from the province of Newfoundland and Labrador, Canada. I have read your two books, **The God Chasers** and **The God Catchers**, and I want to let you know that I have found your books to be the most inspiring and fascinating books I have ever read next to the most important book and Word of God, the Bible. I started reading **The God Chasers** first, and I could not put it down. Then I ordered the second book, **The God Catchers**. I have passed the books around to my friends, and they, too, really enjoyed reading them. I have felt the way that you have, but I could not really put into words the way I have been feeling. But you certainly expressed everything that I have wanted to say in your book.*

—Daphne E.

✑   ✑

*It's a great opportunity I feel, to communicate with you my experience after reading **The God Chasers**. My concept of God changed after I read your book. All glory to God. I live in Abu Dhabi, the capital of United Arab Emirates. In fact, my pastor gave me your book. The book from beginning to end is so wonderful! But the place where you explained about Mary Magdalene and Esther touched my heart. I would read and cry. Wherever God's conviction came, I would kneel down and pray. My spiritual life took a complete U-turn. Instead of the gifts, I started to concentrate on the Giver. Prayer life is no longer a struggle for me. I enjoy being with Him. Now I am just like the Shulamite lady in Song of Solomon searching for my Beloved. Our church also has caught the fire. Always when I bend my knees for prayers, I whisper a prayer for you and your* *ministry because your book was a tremendous blessing. We are praying for a revival in this land. You might know that this is a Muslim land. Restrictions are there. Please pray that God will open a way.*

—Jolly V.

Ask Some Questions

1. Look at the thesaurus list above. How can we dismantle those things (our glory) in order to better minister to God?

2. We're all familiar with the story of Mary's alabaster box. Could anyone ever accuse you of extravagant worship?

    Why might the disciples have "missed" the worship in what Mary was doing?

    What are the "alabaster boxes" in your life?

3. "Son, the services that you consider your favorite services and those I favor are not the same services." When you first read that statement, what do you think?

    What is the difference between entertaining man and entertaining God in a church service? How would those church services look different?

Endnotes

1. See Phil. 3:5-6.

2. See Ps. 91:1.

3. I borrowed this phrase, "disabled heart," from John Bunyan, *The Acceptable Sacrifice*, or *The Excellency of a Broken Heart* (Sterling, VA: Grace Abounding Ministries, Inc., 1988; reprinted from the 1958 edition of Mr. O.G. Pearce, The Retreat, Harpendon, Herte, England), 21. John Bunyan uncovered this truth in this, his last book. He considered *The Acceptable Sacrifice* to be the culmination of his work, more important than any other, including *Pilgrim's Progress*. I would encourage you to read this work if you are at all interested in wrestling with God. It is available from GodChasers.network, P.O. Box 3355, Pineville, LA 71361.

4. See Mt. 26:6-7; Mk. 14:3.

5. See Ps. 56:8.

6. See 1 Cor. 11:15.

7. See Is. 64:6.

8. See Is. 64:6.

9. See Jn. 20:17. Three days later, Jesus returned to appear to the rest of the disciples. They could touch Him then, but only after He had completed His mission to the mercy seat.

10. Of course, we know that the death of Jesus was once for all, never to be repeated and forever sealed with His resurrection. My point here is just to say that even if He would have jeopardized His sacrifice for the sake of Mary—which, of course, was impossible—He would have called to her anyway. that's how great the pull of an anointer is on God!

11. See Ps. 51.

Chapter 10

Moses' 1,500-Year Pursuit of God's Glory

You can't seek His face and save your "face"

When God tells us, "You can't see My face," most of us are satisfied that we've done our religious duty and we quickly return to life as usual. When we discover that God's best and deepest treasures require death to self, we often don't pursue Him any further. We don't ask the questions we need to ask to find out *why* His presence doesn't come cheaply. Perhaps it's because we think it is impertinent or we are simply afraid of His answer. Moses persisted. He had learned that *it isn't impertinent to pursue God for His own sake; it is God's greatest desire and delight.*

This burning desire to see God's glory, to see Him face to face, is one of the most important keys to revival, reformation, and the fulfillment of God's purposes on the earth. We need to look closely at the 1,500-year pursuit of God's glory by the ancient patriarch, Moses. As we noted

213

earlier in Chapter 4, when Moses told God, "Show me Your glory," the Lord said, "You can't, Moses. Only dead men can see My face." Fortunately Moses didn't stop there. Unfortunately, the Church did.

It would have been easy for this man to have been satisfied with God's first answer, but he wasn't. Moses wasn't selfish or presumptuous. He wasn't seeking material things or personal fame. He wasn't even seeking miracles or gifts (and Paul even instructed us to seek after the best gifts in his letter to the Corinthians). Moses simply wanted *God*, and that is the greatest gift and blessing we can ever give Him. Yet Moses had to *pursue* Him, and it didn't come easy.

> *And* [Moses] *said, I beseech Thee, **show me Thy glory.***
> *And He said, I will make all My goodness pass before thee, and I will proclaim the name of the Lord before thee; and will be gracious to whom I will be gracious, and will show mercy on whom I will show mercy.*
> *And He said, **Thou canst not see My face: for there shall no man see Me, and live.***
> *And the Lord said, Behold, there is a place by Me, and thou shalt stand upon a rock:*
> *And it shall come to pass, while My glory passeth by, that I will put thee in a clift of the rock, and will cover thee with My hand while I pass by:*
> *And I will take away Mine hand, and **thou shalt see My back parts: but My face shall not be seen*** (Exodus 33:18-23).

By the time Moses had this discussion with God, the Israelites had already turned their backs to run from God when He asked them to draw near on Mount Sinai. It was

Moses who had boldly pressed into the cloud of His presence. In fear and trembling, Israel demanded that Moses and the Aaronic priesthood stand between them and the God they feared because of their sin. Moses often walked into the concealing cloud in the tent of meeting, and somehow he dared to desire even more.

Will We Pursue Public Approval or God?

*W*hile Moses pursued God on a mountaintop on the Israelites' behalf, his brother Aaron, the high priest, yielded to the pressure of public opinion and agreed to make an idolatrous golden calf for the Israelites. Then the people pursued their pleasures in the valley while Moses watched the finger of God inscribe the law onto tablets of stone. It was after this episode that God told Moses He would still allow the Israelites to cross over into the promised land, but they would have to make do with an angel, "...for I will not go up in the midst of thee; for thou art a stiffnecked people: lest I consume thee in the way" (Ex. 33:3). Moses answered:

> ...See, Thou sayest unto me, Bring up this people: and Thou hast not let me know whom Thou wilt send with me. Yet Thou hast said, I know thee by name, and thou hast also found grace in My sight.
> Now therefore, I pray Thee, if I have found grace in Thy sight, show me now Thy way, **that I may know Thee,** that I may find grace in Thy sight: and consider that this nation is Thy people.
> And He said, My presence shall go with thee, and I will give thee rest.
> And he said unto Him, **If Thy presence go not with me, carry us not up hence** (Exodus 33:12-15).

Moses saw and experienced the miracles and super-natural provision of God along with all the other Israelites. *So has the modern Church*, at least in a small measure.

Most of us would have leaped at the chance to have the verbal strength and promise of God to go with us wherever we go. But who is to say we even know where we should go? Moses wisely answered, "If You don't lead, I'm not going anywhere." *He understood that it was "good" to have God go with you, but that it was "better" to go with God.* God negotiated with Moses, "I will give you rest." I think the New Testament fulfillment of God's "rest" to the Church is found in the supernatural gifts of the Spirit that enable us to effectively train and minister to the Body with a minimum of human effort. In Isaiah 28:11-12 the Scriptures say, "For with stammering lips and another tongue will He speak to this people. To whom He said, *This is the rest....*" I believe that the gifts of the Spirit (including tongues) are the "rest" referred to here. God was saying metaphorically, "Moses, I'll give you the gifts, the 'rest',￼" and Moses was saying, "I don't want the gifts; *I want You.*" The Church is so enamored with the gifts of the Spirit that we don't know the Giver of the gifts. We're having so much fun playing with God's gifts that we've even forgotten to thank Him. The best thing we can do as God's kids is to lay down His gifts long enough to go sit in the Father's lap. Seek the Giver, not the gifts! Seek His face, not His hands!

Moses Wanted Habitation, Not Visitation

The Israelites rarely took time to thank God for His mighty acts because they were too busy compiling "want lists" and official complaints connected with their physical and personal desires. The vast majority of us today have done the same thing. Moses, however, wanted something more. He had experienced the miracles. He had heard God's voice and witnessed His delivering power. More than any other person alive at that time, Moses had even experienced the manifest presence of God in measure, in temporary visitation. But everything he saw and experienced in God told him that there was *far more* just waiting for him beyond the cloud. He longed for more than *visitation*; his soul longed for *habitation*. He wanted more than just seeing God's finger or hearing His voice speaking from a cloud or a burning bush. He had gone beyond fear to love, and God's abiding presence had become his consuming desire. That is why he begged God in Exodus 33:18:

"I beseech Thee, show me Thy glory."

He wanted to see God's face! God was quick to grant Moses' request for Israel. His presence would still go before the people, but He didn't grant Moses' most urgent request directly. First God said that He would cause all His goodness to pass before Moses, and that He knew Moses by name. But then the Lord explained to Moses, "Thou canst not see My face: for there shall no man see Me, and live" (Ex. 33:20). That statement appears to be a closed case, but Moses somehow sensed "there was a way." The Lord told Moses, "Look, you can't see My face, but *there is a place by Me* where you can see Me as I disappear off in the distance" (see Ex. 33:21-23).

Most people would have been more than happy with that answer, but Moses had tasted the unearthly joy of the Lord's presence and he was acquiring a taste for God that couldn't be satisfied from a "safe" distance. A hunger had been ignited in his being that would drive him to risk death in God's presence to achieve satisfaction. That hunger was destined to span 1,500 years and death itself to find fulfillment.

The Lord told Moses to "present himself" to Him on top of the mountain the next morning, and He would hide him in the cleft of a rock while His glory passed by. Now that is an interesting procedure. God was saying, "Now before I ever get there, I am going to reach forward in time to cover you with My hand while I pass by you. After I pass by, I am going to pull My hand away so you can stick your head out and look in the direction I've gone. Then you will see just a little bit of My 'back parts' as I disappear into the distance" (see Ex. 33:22-23).

So God came in His glory at the speed of light or faster to proclaim His divine name and pass by in His glory. As He passed by, He pulled His hand away from the cleft in the rock so Moses could see the backside of His glory disappearing in the distance. Even though this brief revelation came as quickly as a flash of lightning, it made such an impact on Moses that he was able to dictate the Book of Genesis for later generations, the "backside" or the history of God, describing his vision of the creation.

"The Problem Is That You're Still Alive"

*M*oses saw where God had been. He saw God's tracks where He invented and invaded time. Then he was able to retrace history with supernatural insight after that single flash of God's receding glory before his eyes. Even after this experience Moses wanted more, but God's words still remained with him, "You're *alive*, Moses; you can't see My face."

Moses knew that there was a greater purpose behind the tabernacle and everything he had received from God, and he felt a driving need to know God and to see His eternal purpose fulfilled. Moses knew the only way to do it was to look into the face of God. *I've got to see Your glory; I've got to see the finished product.* The hunger in Moses' heart birthed a prayer and a persistence that defied the limits of time, space, and eternity.

If you ever get so hungry for God
that you are in pursuit of Him,
He will do things for you
that He won't do for anybody else.

The conclusion to this story can't be found in the Old Testament. You have to jump ahead 1,500 years or so to a new era and a new covenant to find the end of the hunger that began in Moses' life in the Book of Exodus. Moses had a consuming hunger for God that produced what I call an "unforgettable prayer." Moses' prayer that he see God's glory continued to echo in God's ears every day, every week, and every year over the centuries until the day Jesus spoke to His disciples about going to a mountain in Israel many generations later. That God-birthed prayer from Moses' heart was an eternal thing that knew no limits in time. It didn't die the day Moses took his last breath on earth; it continued to echo through the throne room of God until the moment that prayer was granted.

That moment came late in the earthly ministry of Jesus Christ, on a day when He separated three of His most faithful followers to accompany Him to the top of a high mountain. Jesus had already begun to weed out His disciples with statements like, "For whosoever will save his life shall lose it: and whosoever will lose his life for My sake shall find it" (Mt. 16:25). (That statement still bothers us today because there is "death" in it.)

Jesus had been pouring His life into the disciples, but they seemed to have a serious problem understanding what He was doing and why. They liked His teaching, but they rarely seemed to understand it. They loved to see Him work miracles, but they were never able to grasp the greater purpose behind them. The disciples just followed Him around trying to understand a little of what He was doing.

Nearly All Disciples Fall Asleep During Prayer Meetings

On this one day, Jesus took three disciples with Him to the mountain and began to pray. I am convinced that the disciples of the first century weren't any different from the disciples of the twentieth century, because all of them seem to fall asleep during prayer meetings.

> *And it came to pass about an eight days after these sayings, He took Peter and John and James, and went up into a mountain to pray.*
>
> *And as He prayed, the fashion of His countenance was altered, and His raiment was white and glistering.*
>
> *And, behold, there talked with Him two men, which were Moses and Elias:*
>
> *Who appeared in glory, and spake of His decease which He should accomplish at Jerusalem.*
>
> *But Peter and they that were with Him were heavy with sleep: and when they were awake, **they saw His glory**, and the two men that stood with Him.*
>
> *And it came to pass, as they departed from Him, Peter said unto Jesus, Master, it is good for us to be here: and let us make three tabernacles; one for Thee, and one for Moses, and one for Elias: not knowing what he said.*

While he thus spake, there came a cloud, and over-
shadowed them: and they feared as they entered
into the cloud (Luke 9:28-34).

There's that cloud again. It's almost like, "Uh oh...if
they wake up, they're going to see the 'glory.' Quick, cloud,
cover us."

Did you notice that it was only after the disciples
were asleep that God unzipped the robe of human flesh
that cloaked the glory of God in Jesus Christ? Today we
refer to that mountain as "the mount of transfiguration"
because the Bible says the Lord's garments became "white
and glistering." The original Greek term for glistering, *ex-*
astrapto, "signifies to flash like lightning, gleam, be radi-
ant."[1] While the disciples were sleeping, Jesus Christ was
there alone as His glory was being revealed, bathing the
earth with the preexistent light of the glory of God—in a
lightning-like robe!

It Is Time for You to See Me Now

*I*n that moment, it is as if He said, "Okay now,
Michael, Gabriel [the two archangels], *go get*
Moses. It is time for him to see My glory now." In the halls
of Heaven they dusted off Jacob's ladder and extended it to
the earth and Moses walked down to a place where he'd
never been before—the promised land of his people. In his
natural life, Moses was doomed to stand on the wilderness
side of the river Jordan and look into the promised land of
revival without ever participating in it. He had prayed to
see the glory of God, but he could never see it *until after he*
was dead. On this day, 1,500 years after his death, after the
unforgettable prayer of Moses had echoed in God's ears
unceasingly day after day, Moses "the dead man walking"
saw the glory of God unveiled.

You need to understand that even after you die, *your prayers live on.* For 1,500 years the prayer of Moses kept saying, "Show me Your glory. Show me Your glory. Show me Your glory!" until it prodded the very conscience of God. He had to make a divine appointment and set a day when eternity would intersect the limited spheres of time and space. "Moses, *now that you're dead,* I guess I'm going to have to answer that prayer!"

It is for this reason that I get excited when I read about the faithful, persistent prayers of those who went before us. I am stirred in my spirit when I see saints in our day join their fervent prayers with those of Aimee Semple McPherson and of William Seymour, who often stuck his head in the apple crate at Azusa Street to pray for the glory of God to come down.

When the full measure of the gathered prayers of God's people finally reach a crescendoing echo in God's ears, then it becomes too much for Him to wait any longer. He cannot pass by the prayers of the brokenhearted and contrite who seek His face. Finally the day comes when God says from His throne on high, *"That's it."*

That is what happened in Argentina when Dr. Edward Miller and his 50 Bible students began to besiege the throne with prayers of fervent intercession. As we noted earlier, Argentina was a spiritual wasteland in the 1950's as far as Dr. Miller knew. He said he only knew of 600 Spirit-filled believers in the entire nation at that time, but some Bible students in a tiny Bible school began to intercede. They began to weep with supernatural, Spirit-birthed compassion for a nation that didn't even know they existed. God thundered the Argentinian answer. The same thing is happening in places around the globe where revival is breaking out like unquenchable wildfire. We're tired of doing things man's way. We want "Father" to show up, even if we have to die in brokenness and repentance to see it happen.

Moses prayed, "Show me Thy glory," and it took 1,500 years for that prayer to be answered. There were three sleepy disciples who benefited from Moses' unforgettable prayer, but they fell into the same trap that threatens the sleepy Church today. Moses stepped onto that mountain that day and saw the unveiled glory of God. As he was leaving, the disciples finally woke up—just as it was all fading and Jesus was saying good-bye. Yet the three men were so overcome by the briefest glimpse of that fading glory that they wanted to build three monuments right on the spot and camp there! But God the Father intervened from Heaven and said, "No, this isn't even what it's all about yet. You haven't seen anything yet" (see Lk. 9:34-35).

Sometimes We Can Stop Short

Some of us seem to thrive on the momentary revelations of God when He wants us to press in for His secret things. He loves to honor the prayers of persistent pursuers like Moses, but He will actually stop our attempts to build monuments to partial and incomplete revelations of His glory—especially ones that we never paid for with our prayers and death on the altar of brokenness. We like things to come quickly, easily, and cheaply—*microwave revival.* God knows that such things never produce godly character in us. He says:

> *...If any man will come after Me, let him deny himself, and take up his cross, and follow Me.*
> *For whosoever will save his life shall lose it: and whosoever will lose his life for My sake shall find it.*
> *For what is a man profited, if he shall gain the whole world, and lose his own soul? or what shall a*

man give in exchange for his soul? (Matthew 16:24-26).

I have feebly tried to explain the unexplainable, but all I know is this: *"The more I die, the closer God gets."* I don't know how much of God you know or have, but He will reveal *more* of Himself to you if you are willing to die to yourself. Paul the apostle said he knew a man (himself) who was caught up into the third heaven in Second Corinthians 12:2. This apostle didn't merely know "about" God; he *knew God.* How did he gain that intimate knowledge? He said, "I die daily" (see 1 Cor. 15:31).

Many modern saints spend a lot of time looking for shortcuts to God's glory. We *want the gain without the pain.* We want revival in our cities, but we don't want to hear anyone tell us that revival only comes when people are hungry, when "vicarious intercessors" repent for sins they never committed on behalf of people they've never met. Paul said, "For I could wish that myself were accursed from Christ for my brethren, my kinsmen according to the flesh" (Rom. 9:3).

You are reading this book by divine appointment. Somewhere, somehow, an unforgettable prayer is being answered today. But it could be that you are avoiding death and you're running from the altar of sacrifice that God has placed before you. (Don't worry, it is true of *all* of us.) The greatest blessing doesn't come from God's hand; it comes from His face in intimate relationship. You find the true source of all power when you finally see Him and *know* Him in His glory.

The More You Die, the Closer He Can Come

*N*ow let me tell you the good news beyond the altar of death and brokenness. While all flesh dies in His glory, all that is of the Spirit *lives forever* in His glory. That part of your being that really wants to live can live forever, but something about your flesh has to die. Let me put it this way: *Your flesh holds back the glory of God.* The God of Moses is willing to reveal Himself to you today, but it is not going to be a "cheap" blessing. You're going to have to lay down and die, and *the more you die, the closer He can come.*

You need to forget about the opinions and expectations of those around you. You need to lay aside every idea of what the "normal religious protocol" may be. God has only one protocol for the flesh: *death.* God is out to redefine the Church. He is sending His fire to burn away everything that isn't from Him anyway, so you have nothing to lose...but your flesh. God isn't looking for religious people; He's looking for people who are hot after His heart. He wants people who want Him, who want the Blesser more than the blessings.

We can seek for His blessing and play with His toys, or we can say, "No, Father, we don't just want the blessings; we want *You.* We want You to come close. Touch our eyes. Touch our hearts and ears. Change us, Lord. We are tired of the way we are. We understand that if we can change, then our city and nation can change."

Are You Going to Let Him Get Close?

I believe that this generation is very close to revival, but I don't want to simply watch as God passes down the street to go somewhere else where people really *want Him.* "It's going to happen *somewhere,* but if not us, *who,* Lord? We aren't satisfied with Your gifts, as wonderful as they are. We want You." The equation for revival is still the same:

> *If My people, which are called by My name,* **shall**
> **humble themselves** [die on the altar of repentance],

*and pray, **and seek My face** [instead of just re-vival or momentary visitations], and turn from their wicked ways; then will I hear from heaven, and will forgive their sin, and will heal their land* (2 Chronicles 7:14).

"Father, we seek Your face."

As God redefines the Church, it is highly likely that the Church that emerges from the cloud of His glory will look very different from what you and I think the Church should look like. This will happen because God is repossessing the Church and drawing it close to Him.

Will we dare to draw close to His glory? God really wanted the children of Israel to come up and receive the Ten Commandments directly from Him along with Moses. But they ran from God's presence. The Church is in danger of doing the same thing today. We can take the risk of something dying in us as we dare to draw close to His glory, or we can turn and run back to our traditions of men and the safety of religious legalism and man-operated church services. *Seeker-friendly is fine; Spirit-friendly is fire!*

Let's create a comfort zone for God and a discomfort zone for man by repentant worship. Our churches are more comfortable for man, plush with padding, than they are comfortable for God, stripped of flesh!

The Israelites literally isolated and insulated themselves from God's intimate presence because of their fear of death. Moses, on the other hand, drew near to the thick darkness concealing God's glory. It is time for the Church to truly embrace the cross of Jesus. Our hunger must propel us beyond the death of the flesh into the life and light of God's glory. It is the destiny of the Church of the living God. But it will only happen when we lay down the security of the "new covenant law" of religious practice and carefully controlled "supernatural" visitations for the apparent uncertainty and risk of living face to face with our supernatural God.

God doesn't want us to turn away from His glory so we can build pitiful monuments to a momentary revelation we never paid for with our tears. *Salvation is a free gift, but God's glory will cost us everything.* He wants us to press in and live in His perpetual habitation of glory. He wants us to be so saturated with His presence and glory that we carry His presence with us everywhere we go in this life. This may be the only way the unspeakable glory of God will find its way to the shopping malls, hair style salons, and grocery stores of our nation.

This is the way God's glory is destined to cover the whole earth. It has to start somewhere. The fountains of flesh have to be broken up, as well as the windows of Heaven opened up, for the glory to begin to flow like a river and cover the earth. Jesus said, "Out of [your] belly shall flow rivers of living water" (Jn. 7:38b). We will have to be totally sold out to Him if His glory is going to cover the earth.

The difference between the anointing and the glory is the difference between God's hands and His face, and the path to the glory of God takes us right up to the altar where we must lay everything down and die. In the end, we will find ourselves face to face with God as a nation of "dead men walking," in possession of His glory. Nothing else is needed; nothing else is necessary. Once God's children lay down their toys and crawl into the Father's lap to seek His face, the House of Bread will once again overflow with fresh bread and every good gift. *The hungry will find the eternal satisfaction that they've always longed for.*

He will not frustrate us. God will allow Himself to be caught by us. As a father playing tag with his child allows himself to be caught by the laughing, loving child, so too will the heavenly Father allow Himself to be caught. In fact, just when you would tire in despair, He will turn and catch you. He wants to be "captured" by our love. He eagerly awaits the laughing, loving encounter. He has missed those times with man since the Garden. Intuitively, God chasers have known this. *They were willing to chase the "uncatchable," knowing the "impossible" would catch them.* In fact, one famous God chaser wrote this:

> *I follow after, if that I may apprehend that for which also I am apprehended of Christ Jesus* (Philippians 3:12b).

Paul caught Him!
So can you! Come join the company of God chasers! The "chase" is on....

➤ Notes from those on the chase ➤

*I am a 50-year-old, single, wheelchair-bound Christian. I will be seven years old in Christ on October 10, and in the light of what happened on September 11, I could not sleep and went to Wal-Mart at 4 a.m. I purchased your book, **The Daily Chase**...I looked for the CD in the back. I listened to it over and over...I can't begin to thank you for the temporary relief that it enabled me to have...to stay focused on what is really important...JESUS...Thank you for the changes that your books have had on my life...teaching me that nothing is more important than His presence.*

—Jeanette C.

➤   ➤

*My name is DeLeon R. I have spent my entire life as a gospel-recording artist. A friend gave **The God Chasers** to my husband and me. In our busy lives, we put the book in our library and did not think about it again. Then one day we were sitting around the dinner table and a friend of ours, Kirk F., mentioned **The God Chasers.** He said it was such a wonderful book and that we had to read it.*

I remembered having the book in our library. I got it out and began to read it. Wow! What an incredible book! My husband, Gary S., a baseball player for the LA Dodgers, began to read it. He could not put it down. He would be traveling with the Dodgers and would call me to share something great about the book.

Because of the impact the book had on us personally, we bought more than 15 copies and gave them to Gary's teammates. It is hard to believe there could be such anointing in the pages of one book. It made such an impression on our lives that we keep telling our friends they have to read it.

Thank you, Tommy, for such a life-changing book.

—DeLeon R.

Ask Some Questions

1. The hunger of one person—Moses—changed the history of a nation. What could one truly hungry person do today in a church, city, or region?

   What would a "Moses-sized" hunger look like today?

2. Can we be truly hungry without a prayer life? How is your prayer life?

3. What does this statement mean: "Salvation is a free gift, but God's glory will cost us everything?"

   We long for a Moses-style encounter without paying the price. What is the price, and how do we pay it?

4. Read Second Corinthians 3:18. What happens to us when
    we do see His face? Do you want to be changed from glory
    to glory?

    What must you do to allow that change to happen?

Endnote

1. W.E. Vine, *Vine's Expository Dictionary of Old and New Testament Words* (Old Tappan, NJ: Fleming H. Revell Company, 1981), as listed under "dazzling," Vol. 1, 272.

GODChasers.network

GodChasers.network is the ministry of Tommy and Jeannie Tenney. Their heart's desire is to see the presence and power of God fall—not just in churches, but on cities and communities all over the world.

How to contact us:

By Mail:

GodChasers.network
P.O. Box 3355
Pineville, Louisiana 71361
USA

By Phone:

Voice:	318.44CHASE (318.442.4273)
Fax:	318.442.6884
Orders:	888.433.3355

By Internet:

E-mail:	GodChaser@GodChasers.net
Website:	www.GodChasers.net

Join Today

When you join the **GodChasers.network** we'll send you a free teaching tape!

If you share in our vision and want to stay current on how the Lord is using GodChasers.network, please add your name to our mailing list. We'd like to keep you updated on what the Spirit is saying through Tommy. We'll also send schedule updates and make you aware of new resources as they become available.

Sign up by calling or writing to:

Tommy Tenney
GodChasers.network
P.O. Box 3355
Pineville, Louisiana 71361-3355
USA

318-44CHASE (318.442.4273)
or sign up online at http://www.GodChasers.net/lists/

We regret that we are only able to send regular postal mailings to certain countries at this time. If you live outside the U.S. you can still add your postal address to our mailing list—you will automatically begin to receive our mailings as soon as they are available in your area.

E-mail Announcement List

If you'd like to receive information from us via e-mail, just provide an e-mail address when you contact us and let us know that you want to be included on the e-mail announcement list!

BOOKS BY

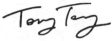

THE GOD CHASERS
$12.00 plus $4.50 S&H

What is a God Chaser? A person whose hunger exceeds his reach…a person whose passion for God's presence presses him to chase the impossible in hopes that the uncatchable might catch him.

The great GodChasers of the Scripture—Moses, Daniel, David—see how they were driven by hunger born of tasting His goodness. They had seen the invisible and nothing else satisfied. Add your name to the list. Come join the ranks of the God Chasers.

CHASING GOD, SERVING MAN
$17.00 plus $4.50 S&H

Using the backdrop of Bethany and the house of Mary and Martha, Tommy Tenney biblically explores new territory. The revolutionary concepts in this book can change your life. You will discover who you really are (and unlock the secret of who "they" really are)!

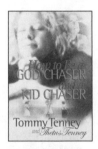

HOW TO BE A GOD CHASER AND A KID CHASER
$12.00 plus $4.50 S&H

Combining years of both spiritual passion and practical parenting, Tommy Tenney and his mother, Thetus Tenney, answer the questions that every parent has. Helping them are the touching and sometimes humorous insights of such Christian greats as Dutch and Ceci Sheets, Cindy Jacobs and others. You'll have to open this book to discover.

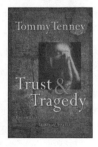

TRUST AND TRAGEDY
$7.00 plus $4.50 S&H

When tragedy strikes, your desperate hunt for hope in the secular forest will be futile. The hunters invariably go home emptyhanded and brokenhearted, because humanity doesn't have the answers. Jesus gave us the key in one of the most direct and unequivocal statements ever made: "I am the way, the truth, and the life. No one comes to the Father, except through me." This book is a signpost along the way, through the truth, and to the life. If life is what you need, trust in God will take you there.

GodChasers.network
P.O. Box 3355, Pineville, Louisiana 71361-3355
318-44CHASE (318.442.4273)
www.GodChasers.net

VIDEOTAPE ALBUMS BY

Tommy Tenney

GOING HOME FROM A FUNERAL
Video ~~$20.00~~ $10.00 plus $4.50 S&H

Our country is now in a crisis. Some things will never be the same. Our national mentality is as if we are "going home from a funeral." We are no longer in the orderly, controlled funeral procession. Cars have scattered, taking their own routes back to individual homes and routines. The lights are off and reality hits.

FOLLOW THE MAN ON THE COLT
Video $20.00 plus $4.50 S&H

From humility to authority.... If we learn to ride the colt of humility, then we qualify to ride on the stallion of authority.

(This new video helps us understand that we all start this journey crawling—which strenghthens us to walk—that empowers us to run—and rewards us to ride!) Enjoy this great teaching by Tommy Tenney on following the Man on the colt. It will change the way you see the obstacles put in your path! Remember, there is never a testimony without a test!

BROWNSVILLE WILDFIRE SERIES, VOL. 1
"Born to Be a Worshiper"
Video $20.00 plus $4.50 S&H

God would rather hear the passionate praises of His children than the perfection of heavenly worship. It isn't about how good we are as singers, or how skilled we are as musicians. It isn't about singing catchy choruses with clever words. It's all about GOD, and if we'll let our guard down and allow ourselves to truly worship Him, we'll find that He's closer than we ever imagined. If you've been born into God's kingdom, then you were born to be a worshiper! It's time to do the very thing that we were created for!

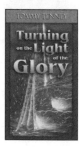

TURNING ON THE LIGHT OF THE GLORY
Video $20.00 plus $4.50 S&H

Tommy deals with turning on the light of the glory and presence of God, and he walks us through the necessary process and ingredients to potentially unleash what His Body has always dreamed of.

GodChasers.network
P.O. Box 3355, Pineville, Louisiana 71361-3355
318-44CHASE (318.442.4273)
www.GodChasers.net

AUDIOTAPE ALBUMS BY

WHAT'S THE FIGHT ABOUT?
(audiotape album) $20 plus $4.50 S&H

Tape 1 — Preserving the Family: God's special gift to the world is the family! If we don't preserve the family, the church is one generation from extinction. God's desire is to heal the wounds of the family from the inside out.

Tape 2 — Unity in the Body: An examination of the levels of unity that must be respected and achieved before "Father let them be one" becomes an answered prayer!

Tape 3 — "IF you're throwing dirt, you're just losing ground!" In "What's the Fight About?" Tommy invades our backyards to help us discover our differences are not so different after all!

FANNING THE FLAMES
(audiotape album) $20 plus $4.50 S&H

Tape 1 — The Application of the Blood and the Ark of the Covenant: Most of the churches in America today dwell in an outer-court experience. Jesus made atonement with His own blood, once and for all, and the veil in the temple was rent from top to bottom.

Tape 2 — A Tale of Two Cities—Nazareth & Nineveh: What city is more likely to experience revival: Nazareth or Nineveh? You might be surprised....

Tape 3 — The "I" Factor: Examine the difference between *ikabod* and *kabod* ("glory"). The arm of flesh cannot achieve what needs to be done. God doesn't need us; we need Him.

KEYS TO LIVING THE REVIVED LIFE
(audiotape album) $20 plus $4.50 S&H

Tape 1 — Fear Not: To have no fear is to have faith, and perfect love casts out fear, so we must establish the trust of a child in our loving Father.

Tape 2 — Hanging in There: Have you ever been tempted to give up, quit, and throw in the towel? This message is a word of encouragement for you.

Tape 3 — Fire of God: Fire purges the sewer of our souls and destroys the hidden things that would cause disease. Learn the way out of a repetitive cycle of seasonal times of failure.

PURSUING HIS PRESENCE
(audiotape album) $20 plus $4.50 S&H

Tape 1 — Transporting the Glory: There comes a time when God wants us to grow to another level of maturity. For us, that means walking by the Spirit rather than according to the flesh.

Tape 2 — Turning on the Light of the Glory: Tommy walks us through the process of unleashing what the Body of Christ has always dreamed of: getting to the Glory!

Tape 3 — Building a Mercy Seat: In worship, we create an appropriate environment in which the presence of God can dwell. The focus of the church needs to be shifted from simply dusting the furniture to building the mercy seat.

GodChasers.network
P.O. Box 3355, Pineville, Louisiana 71361-3355
318-44CHASE (318.442.4273)
www.GodChasers.net

Run With Us!

Become a GodChasers.network Monthly Revival Partner

Two men, a farmer and his friend, were looking out over the farmer's fields one afternoon. It was a beautiful sight—it was nearly harvest time, and the wheat was swaying gently in the wind. Inspired by this idyllic scene, the friend said, "Look at God's provision!" The farmer replied, "You should have seen it when God had it by Himself!"

This humorous story illustrates a serious truth. Every good and perfect gift comes from Him: but we are supposed to be more than just passive recipients of His grace and blessings. We must never forget that only God can cause a plant to grow—but it is equally important to remember that *we are called to do our part in the sowing, watering, and harvesting.*

When you sow seed into this ministry, you help us reach people and places you could never imagine. The faithful support of individuals like you allows us to send resources, free of charge, to many who would otherwise be unable to obtain them. Your gifts help us carry the gospel all over the world—including countries that have been closed to evangelism. Would you prayerfully consider partnering with us? As a small token of our gratitude, our Revival Partners who send a monthly gift of $30 or more receive a teaching tape every month. This ministry could not survive without the faithful support of partners like you!

Stand with me now—so we can run together later!

In Pursuit,

Tommy Tenney

Tommy Tenney

**Become a Monthly Revival Partner
by calling or writing to:**

Tommy Tenney/GodChasers.network
**P.O. Box 3355
Pineville, Louisiana 71361-3355
318.44CHASE (318.442.4273)**

Additional copies of this book and other
book titles from DESTINY IMAGE are
available at your local bookstore.

For a complete list of our titles,
visit us at www.destinyimage.com
Send a request for a catalog to:

Destiny Image® Publishers, Inc.

P.O. Box 310
Shippensburg, PA 17257-0310

*"Speaking to the Purposes of God for This
Generation and for the Generations to Come"*